# Pixie Annat

# champion *of* nurses

# Pixie Annat
# champion *of* nurses

**Colleen Ryan Clur**

UQP

Dedicated to my mother, Phyllis Ryan,
and all the mothers of the world

First published 2015 by
University of Queensland Press,
PO Box 6042, St Lucia, Queensland, 4067, Australia

www.uqp.com.au



Custom Publisher: Lynn P Bryan
Project Manager: Stan Lamond
Designer: Stan Lamond
Editor: Marie-Louise Taylor
Proofreader: Dannielle Viera
Cover Photograph: Ray Cash
Printed in China by 1010 Printing International

Cataloguing-in-Publication Data
*National Library of Australia*
Cataloguing-in-publication data is available at http://catalogue.nla.gov.au

ISBN 978 0 70225372 0 (pbk)
ISBN 978 0 70225575 5 (pdf)
ISBN 978 0 70225576 2 (epub)
ISBN 978 0 70225577 9 (kindle)

University of Queensland Press uses papers that are natural, renewable and recyclable products made from wood grown in sustainable forests. The logging and manufacturing processes conform to the environmental regulations of the country of origin.

# Contents

# Introduction

On 18 November 2014, Pixie Annat stood proudly on the campus of St Andrew's War Memorial Hospital in Brisbane to receive a UnitingCare Queensland Moderator's Medal for outstanding community service. It was recognition of her contribution not only to St Andrew's but also to many other organisations that help the sick, the aged and the homeless. The day was a special one for Pixie, not least because she shared it with her cherished confidante and best friend, twin sister Ellen, herself a long-standing volunteer at St Andrew's.

The award ceremony came almost 50 years after Pixie first strode into the hospital to begin working as matron. She would go on to become the hospital's longest-serving CEO, retiring in 1992, and remained very much part of the St Andrew's family as one of its committed volunteers.

Pixie has always fought hard for her beliefs. In her long career before and during her time at St Andrew's, she campaigned for – and helped achieve – better resourcing, training and recognition of nurses as healthcare professionals.

She has been very generous in entrusting her story to me. She had one concern, that she would be seen as drawing attention to her achievements, and she emphasised that there were many colleagues who also championed nurses and nurse education. These women in Queensland include Topsy Moffett, Joan Godfrey and Bartz Schultz, to name but a few.

Pixie's sharp wit, and her ability to recall names and events from many years ago, gave life to this book. Memory is, of course, selective and imperfect – so I hope readers will forgive any errors and enjoy Pixie's story as much as I have enjoyed writing it.

# Acknowledgments

I had a great deal to learn about the world of nurses and hospitals. In particular, I would like to acknowledge Dr Sam (JSD) Mellick for his account of the history of St Andrew's War Memorial Hospital and Helen Gregory for her outstanding histories of the Royal Brisbane Hospital.

I would like to thank Pixie's sister, Ellen Murr, for her insights, and all of Pixie's friends and colleagues who made themselves available for interviews: Mary Abbot, Val French, Meg Gagen, Michael Gardner, Rosemary Hay, Cheryl Herbert, Glennis Hinton, Marie Jameson, Bernice Killen, Sandra Kjellgren, Sam Mellick, Marion Mitchell, Rhyl Row, Fran Ryan, Cluny Seager, Claudia Sharpe, Linda Shields, Jeanette Warwick, Jennifer West, Joy Wilson and Bernard Yorke.

Thank you to my husband, Neill Clur, who was patient with me as I spent many hours untangling Pixie's complex story. Bonnie Harrison provided invaluable help, including transcribing interviews and sourcing photographs. Thank you to editor Marie-Louise Taylor and designer Stan Lamond for their expertise, and to Jennifer Moran and Helen Chryssides for their words of encouragement.

Finally, thank you to St Andrew's War Memorial Hospital for supporting the publication of this book.

## Chapter 1

# Hard Times and Childhood Dreams

## 1930–1945

Pixie Annat is a born storyteller. She has a tale for every occasion, and there is no better place to start than where her story begins at Palmwoods, North Coast Line, Queensland.

She and her twin sister, Ellen, were born on 18 March 1930 in the small Palmwoods Hospital that served the rural township tucked into the eastern foothills of the Blackall Range.

'My father walked from our farm on the side of the Montville Range to the hospital. He looked at both of us lying in the crib and said to my mum, "The little one looks like a Pixie!"

'Mum said, "Then that's what we'll call her".

'I wasn't christened Pixie, but I have never been called anything else since the day I was born. I had a turned-up nose, a pointed chin and I was quite a bit smaller than my sister, Ellie.'

This first story is vintage Pixie. It reveals her sense of humour and features three characters central to her life story: her twin, Ellen (Ellie), her mother, Madoline, and her father, James (Jim).

Pixie, christened Isobel Mary, and Ellen Madoline were the only daughters born to Jim and Madoline, seven years after the arrival of Donald (Don). Don was another main character: her much-loved sibling, already living his own life by the time Pixie was fully conscious of her own identity.

The area known as Palmwoods, with its thick forests rich with red cedar, white cedar, bunya pine and hoop pine, was for centuries home to the Gubi Gubi people. As European settlement expanded in the 19th century, it was first called Merriman's Flat then Palmwoods, after the plentiful endemic piccabeen palms. The fertile land and geography of the area helped shape its history. Located 90 kilometres north of Brisbane and 16 kilometres inland from the coast, since the turn of the century Palmwoods had been an important hub for transporting timber, and later dairy products and fruit and vegetables, to Australian markets.

The children grew up on the family's small farm, 3 kilometres from the Palmwoods settlement. Don had been born in Brisbane, but for her confinement when she was expecting the twins, their mother went to the Palmwoods Hospital, where she was well known by its two nurses and doctor.

Madoline had won the gold medal for theory and practice as a third-year nurse in 1920 at the Brisbane Hospital, a year and a half before her marriage to Jim. Her Palmwoods Hospital friends sometimes asked Madoline for a medical opinion. She enjoyed such discussions, and about once a month she would take their horse, Panshine, and the sulky to Palmwoods, and she always stopped in for morning tea with Sister Malone and Sister Perry. The private hospital, a converted old home opposite the post office, had opened in 1924, and for 20 years it served the approximately 400 Palmwoods townsfolk and 300 others who lived on surrounding farms. The doctor for most of that time was Dr Harold Power, who served in World War I.

The Annat family farmed in Palmwoods between the two world wars, in a time when most people were poor. This taught the children to be thrifty, and they understood from an early age that the best way to get by was to work hard and lend a hand to others when you could.

Jim (James Whamond) Annat had first taken up farming when he returned to Brisbane after serving in the Great War. Born on 29 January 1891 in Charters Towers in North Queensland, Jim was the eldest of five children. His father, also James Whamond Annat who was born to Scottish parents in South Brisbane on 18 December 1864, died fighting in the Anglo-Boer war in August 1900. Following his death, his widow, Isabella (nee Ferguson), who was born on 18 December 1865, and five children – James, David, Hector, Annie and Helen – moved back to Brisbane, where they lived with relatives on the south side of the river in the working-class suburb of Buranda.

At the end of the war, Jim, who had no previous experience as a farmer, bought a farm in partnership with a soldier friend at Victoria Point, where they farmed for a few years. After he married Madoline on 11 June 1921, Jim persuaded his bride to move to the North Coast (later renamed the Sunshine Coast). They secured a loan and bought their 16-hectare farm, complete with a three-bedroom farmhouse, and began the hard work of pineapple and small-crop farming later that year.

Madoline had greater experience with, and no particular fondness for, farm life. Born in the Brisbane suburb of Sandgate on 7 April 1895, she had grown up on a dairy farm outside Crow's Nest on Queensland's Darling Downs.

'Mother decided that she would start nursing, because she didn't want to be on a dairy farm. So she went into Toowoomba Hospital to see what they had there in the way of training. The first thing she saw was one of the nurses down on her knees scrubbing the floor, and Mum decided she was not going to that hospital. She came down to Brisbane for an interview and then she started training in 1916 at the Brisbane Hospital. She was clever and was proud to have been the gold medallist.'

Madoline often spoke of her years spent training at the Brisbane Hospital, and Pixie drank in these stories, interested in the anecdotes about her mother and her friends. It was a time when nurses' daily shifts were long, pay was low and working conditions were poor. While Brisbane Hospital nurses might not have been required to scrub floors, they nevertheless performed many domestic duties like cooking, cleaning wards, making beds and sewing – apart from caring for their patients. After she married, Madoline gave up her nursing career – married women were not allowed to continue to work in public hospitals, and working as a nurse in Palmwoods was impractical because of limited transport.

Life in the 1920s in rural Queensland settlements like Palmwoods was basic. With no electricity, Madoline cooked all meals on the farmhouse wood stove and they used kerosene lamps for lighting. They stored perishable food in a hanging safe – later the family acquired an ice chest, cooled by blocks of ice made in town and delivered by the butcher on Fridays. This was Pixie and Ellie's favourite day of the week, because they looked forward to treats like pork sausages that came tied up with the package of ice.

There was also no running water; that came from a rainwater tank and from the creek that ran through the farm. They washed laundry in tubs, and they used an outside copper pot to boil heavily soiled clothes before wringing out all the washing by hand and hanging it out to dry in the hot Queensland sun.

'The farm itself was very productive, so we grew pineapples and pawpaw on the upper slopes and small crops like tomatoes and cucumbers on the creek flats that went through our farm. The creek always ran. We had a swimming hole there, and Ellie and I would throw two pebbles in to see if anything moved. If nothing moved, we thought that it meant there were no black snakes. We would dive in if nothing moved, otherwise we would shoot up to the house to our mum like rockets.'

On the farm, Pixie and Ellie had a range of jobs, like carrying morning and afternoon tea to their father and any other workmen who were helping out. One of the problems Jim and Madoline confronted running the farm was getting enough money for their fruit and vegetables. For years, factory canneries were unreliable about accepting produce, and prices paid for pineapples were heartbreakingly low. In spite of these trials, the Annat family managed to earn a living. During the Depression, it was common to see swagmen looking for work, and if they passed by the Annat farm they were always given a meal with the family. They would offer to do some work in return for the meal, but Jim, not wanting to delay them, would politely decline and advise them to keep on walking the 6 kilometres up to Montville, where they could get more help.

Ironically, a positive consequence of the Depression was the construction of new roads, which were carved out by relief workers. A new road that ran past the family's farm replaced the perilous Razorback Road from Montville. By 1941, Jim had purchased a utility vehicle to replace their horses, Bessie and Panshine, and this made work on the farm much easier. Ellie and Pixie learned to drive when they were about 13 years old. Sometimes, they helped their father load pineapples onto a slide, ready for them to be packed into the wooden cases assembled by the girls.

'Dad would have all the pineapple cases ready to be loaded for the carter to take to the Palmwoods station. One of Ellie and my jobs was to watch the "top line". The road down the Montville Range was very windy, and there were white railings at the very top road leading to Montville. We could see the trucks coming past these white lines and we'd say, "Allen Brown's is at the white line". By the time this big red truck arrived, Dad had to make sure all the cases of fruit were ready to be loaded.'

The family owned about a dozen cows, and another of the children's jobs was to help with the milking. Pixie and Ellie went with their father many mornings to milk the cows, and after milking led them up to a paddock a short distance from the farmhouse. For breakfast their mother made rather tasteless porridge, and then the twins would set off for school on the family pony. Their daily journey to Palmwoods State School is another classic Pixie story.

'Ellie and I rode Bessie to school from the age of five. If we fell off, we were too small to get back on again. So the farmers on the two miles between our farm and the school knew that if they saw Bessie standing still in the middle of the road – and she wouldn't move, trucks had to go around her – we had fallen off. So one of the farmers would come and put us back on and off we would go again. We had a saddle and a packsaddle on the back of that, which Dad had made – I rode in front to school every day and Ellie was in front going home.'

The family's cattle dog, a black kelpie called Toby, usually accompanied Bessie and the twins on the journey to and from Palmwoods State School. 'On the way home, he would leave us at about the second-last corner before the farm and take off, go in and find Mum, wagging his tail, and she'd say, "The kids are coming, are they, boy?" And Bessie always brought us home safely.'

Pixie and Ellie started Grade One at Palmwoods State School in 1935, and their first teacher was Miss Molly Cranny, who instructed the Grade Ones and Twos. Miss Cranny also rode a horse to school; arriving each day in jodhpurs, she would then change into her work attire while one of her pupils led the horse to the paddock. In their early years at school, the girls wrote on slates, and one of their regular tasks at home was to sharpen their slate pencils on a stone before school the next day. The twins were both bright – and one of Pixie's surviving school reports attests to her quick mind.

Small clues to Pixie's personality were already evident in snippets of news from the local newspaper. In the *Nambour Chronicle and North Coast Advertiser* of September 1940, a report on the school children's concert included a comment that ten-year-old Pixie had taken part in a girls versus boys comedy debate: 'Pixie Annat, as president of the meeting, carried out her duties to perfection.'

Rural education in those days operated on an assumption that most children would follow in their parents' footsteps, working on farms or in trades. Subjects included domestic science (for the girls), and agricultural and horticultural subjects. The headmaster, Mr Bernard Bruce, set high academic standards for his pupils, and this enabled Pixie and Ellen to successfully sit the scholarship exam required for entry into high school, situated in Nambour, about 14 kilometres from their farm.

Don, seven years older than the twins, had also attended Nambour State High School. He had moved to Brisbane to work in the Queensland National Bank by the time Ellie and Pixie were nearing the end of their primary school days.

With their brother absent, the girls mostly had each other for company, and a big treat for them was a monthly trip to town to see a Saturday picture show.

Madoline would take the girls to Palmwoods in the horse and sulky, deposit Panshine in the police yard at the top of the hill, and then the three of them would walk to the picture show held in the Memorial Hall. Completed in 1922, the Memorial Hall was erected in honour of the men who had served in World War I. The hall was like many other memorials built with public donations, and it reflected the widespread patriotism of a young Australian nation. It was an important focus for annual Remembrance Day and ANZAC Day services – and it was the social hub of Palmwoods.

The absence of electricity was no deterrent to socialising, and the local travelling picture show man, Mr Hyde, presented the first silent films, known as 'travelling pictures'. He ran a generator from his truck to show the films, and was assisted by two local men who operated the projector.

There was always a matinee and a night showing at the Saturday pictures. Popular films that Pixie recalled were romances like *Mrs Miniver* and westerns like the latest *Hopalong Cassidy* film. The showing commenced with a short film and the newsreels, followed by interval then the feature film. At interval, the nearby corner cafe opened, and not to be left out, the proprietors from the second cafe near the hotel manned a stall in the porch of the hall to serve hungry patrons.

The Memorial Hall was also the venue for the town's fundraising functions, concerts, wedding receptions, Friday night dances and even several balls, including the school fancy dress ball. Pixie and Ellie were regulars at the fancy dress balls, and with their parents occasionally attended 'send-offs' for soldiers. A big social event was the annual debutante ball. At these important social occasions, young ladies were presented to a local dignitary – for years, local Member of Parliament (and later Premier of Queensland) Frank Nicklin and his wife, Georgina (Ina).

Frank Nicklin, like Jim, had served on the Western Front, and after the war he had bought an 8-hectare pineapple farm near Palmwoods as part of the Soldier Settlement Scheme. He was elected to the Queensland Legislative Assembly for the seat of Murrumba in 1932 and became Premier in 1957. He was friendly with Jim Annat, and Pixie recalled him as a dignified man. Little did she know that later in life she would get to know him quite well when she became matron of St Andrew's War Memorial Hospital, Brisbane.

In Palmwoods, in the 1930s, the need for electricity was a hot topic, and Jim often discussed this problem when he met his local MP, Frank. Electricity finally did arrive in Palmwoods in July 1940, but the farmers of the area had to wait much longer before being connected to the grid.

For the Annat family, another important place in the self-contained township of Palmwoods was the Anglican Church, one of four local churches that served the community; it was an era when most people were church-goers. Madoline and her daughters regularly attended church, and Pixie and Ellie attended Sunday school at a local home on the Palmwoods–Montville Road. On Saturdays, the twins went to the Girls' Friendly Society, held at the church. From a very young age, Pixie developed her deep Christian faith, and she maintained this conviction and a close connection to the Anglican Church throughout her life.

The twins were nine years old when the world as they knew it changed forever. On 3 September 1939, Prime Minister Robert Menzies announced to the nation that Australia was at war with Germany. The wartime years brought small communities like Palmwoods closer together, and local men who joined up, including their brother Don, were farewelled at the Memorial Hall.

Military service in defence of 'Queen and Country' was a tradition in the Annat household, and as loyal British subjects they believed that Australia had a duty to help defend the British Empire. The children knew that both their father and grandfather had fought for Great Britain, and while their father seldom discussed the details, these were nevertheless important family stories.

Jim's father, James, had served bravely as a lieutenant in the Third Queensland Mounted Infantry during the second Anglo-Boer war. His contingent departed from Brisbane on 1 March 1900 – less than six months later, James, as part of a contingent of British, Rhodesian, Australian and New Zealand soldiers, died defending the British garrison at Elands River. The family could not have predicted that just over a hundred years later his granddaughter, Pixie, would be invited back to the place where James had died.

In spite of their loyalty to Great Britain, the Annats were naturally worried about sending their only son to war.

Madoline's brother, John Chambers, who had landed at the Gallipoli peninsula, died in 1917 after fighting on the Western Front.

Jim knew from personal experience the realities of war – he was only seven when his father died. Fifteen years later he, too, had enlisted, and with his younger brother David fought at Gallipoli, on the beaches that became known as Anzac Cove. More than 100,000 men were killed during the failed campaign to capture the strategically important northern bank of the

Dardanelles strait. Well over half of the fatalities were Turkish soldiers; the balance were Allied soldiers from the United Kingdom, France, Australia, New Zealand and British India. The loss of more than 8,000 Australians was deeply felt by a young Australian nation, and ANZAC became an integral part of its national identity; over the years Gallipoli also became an important symbol of remembrance for Pixie.

Jim had joined up as a sergeant in the 25th Battalion at Enoggera, Brisbane, in June 1915 and departed Brisbane on board HMAT *A60 Aneus*. They trained in Egypt, before landing in Gallipoli in September 1915 to reinforce the depleted ANZAC troops – but by then a stalemate had developed in the battles against the Turks. Jim and his battalion left Gallipoli in December 1915 as part of the successful Allied evacuation, and after another round of training in Egypt, they landed in France.

For the next three years, Jim served on the Western Front of France and Belgium, and it was during this time that he was awarded a Military Medal for 'conspicuous gallantry and devotion to duty' for his role in the Battle of Menin Road, near Ypres, Belgium, in September 1917. The Battle of Menin Road was part of the Third Battle of Ypres on the Western Front, launched by the British Second Army, which was fighting for control of the Westhoek Ridge east of Ypres.

James Annat's citation read: 'When the officer had been wounded, he took charge of the platoon and rendered valuable assistance in consolidating the position on the left flank of the company. Later, as acting C.S.M. when the Company Commander had been wounded, he did excellent work in company with the only remaining company officer, in carrying out the relief of the company during heavy shell fire. Throughout the whole attack he set a fine example to all ranks and was continually moving amongst the men and inspiring a high standard of courage and duty.'

In 1918, Jim was promoted to lieutenant and he returned to Australia in February 1919.

Jim was an understated man who seldom spoke of his war experiences – nevertheless, his children were conscious of his bravery, physically represented by his medal but also by a permanent injury to his leg.

It was the small things that their father sometimes mentioned about the war, like a parcel from home with a big tin of strawberry jam that was shared up and down the trenches at Gallipoli.

'Everybody had a taste of it', he told his children.

When he did talk about the war, he mentioned the poor food, the boredom – the hours and hours of inactivity between 'stunts' with no radio or any other distractions – and being bogged down in terrible mud for days and days at a time. Jim was no different to tens of thousands of fellow soldiers who faithfully served in the war and then came home to Australia with physical and emotional scars to continue their lives as best they could.

All three of the Annat children respected their father's war service, and so it was that Don was keen to join up.

'When Don came home from Brisbane, back to the farm, and told Mum and Dad that he was going to join up, they spoke it over with him and realised he was determined to go. Later Dad said, "Why don't you go into the army, boy, like I did?"

'Don said, "And go around in all that mud? Not me. When I come back at night I want a dry bed".

'So he chose the air force, but then he ended up with no bed at all after being shot down.'

Don was only 19 when he joined the Royal Australian Air Force. He trained in Canada as a wireless operator and then went to England, where he served in the 460 Squadron of Lancasters – he was to fly 26 sorties over Europe as part of a seven-member heavy bomber aircrew.

Like his father, Don was reticent when talking about his service that included a story of bravery that Pixie knows very well. It is a memory made vivid for the Annat family by its regular recounting.

'Their Lancaster was shot down in 1944 in a night raid over the Courtrai railway yards in Belgium. The pilot, Captain Harold Jopling, put his life at risk to keep the aircraft going after it had been fired on. All seven who were on board the Lancaster survived thanks to Jopling, who is supposed to have said, "If you buggers don't get out, you can fly the damn thing yourselves". My brother was to be the last one out with him, and said, "Let's go, boss". But just as Don was about to jump, he looked and saw that the captain did not have his parachute – Jopling had not stowed it in the right place when they boarded the plane. So Don went back to get the parachute, helped strap him in and then they both jumped. Jopling said afterwards that Don had saved his life and recommended him for a bravery medal. But he was not awarded a medal because there were no other witnesses.

'We asked Don what was the first thing he did when he landed. He said he buried the parachute because the Germans knew if there was a crash or a plane on fire there could be survivors, and they would be looking for them.

'So he buried the parachute in a little wood and stayed hidden for a day in a hedge. The next morning he showed himself to a farmer, which was a risk. This farmer's 85-year-old mother, who was involved in the Resistance, helped him. They both rode bicycles in the middle of the night and she led him safely to France. Don occasionally talked about it and thought about it. He said to me a few years ago, "I often wonder whether that old lady got home safely".'

In France, and separated from his fellow airmen, Don joined the French Resistance. He remained with them until after the Allied forces landed at Dunkirk and began the liberation of France. Don was missing for 14 weeks before Allied soldiers located him; he was then sent back to England.

It was an anxious wait, far away in Palmwoods – and the news of a 'Palmwoods airman missing' was published in the *Nambour Chronicle and North Coast Advertiser* in August 1944.

'Mother and Dad, when they'd go down to milk the cows in the afternoon, would always say to us, "Listen to the four o'clock news". We had an old radio with a huge battery, and at four o'clock they would always announce how many aircraft had gone out and how many had failed to return. We had been told by telegram that Don's plane had been shot down – families were always advised immediately. But we never knew where he was. We always felt that if we didn't hear anything, it was possibly good news.

'Miss Dorothy Grimes, our school teacher and the deputy principal in Nambour, called us out of class one day. Our parents had received a telegram informing them that Donald had returned to England. Mum rang our school from Palmwoods, and so Miss Grimes gave us the news: "Don is safe in England".'

Miss Grimes was more than merely a messenger – she had taught Don and many of his fellow classmates who had left Queensland to fight in the war.

The entry of the United States into World War II after the Japanese bombing of Pearl Harbor in December 1941 had an unlikely positive consequence for the pineapple farmers of Palmwoods. American and other Allied troops had to be fed, so there was a spike in demand for the Annats' main crop, pineapples, and they got a better price from the canning factories.

'Sometimes before the war, Dad would get a letter in the mail saying, "Please send cheque to cover freight". They wouldn't have got enough money at the market in Sydney to even cover the freight. When the war came, we used to get telegrams saying, "Send on. Send on". There was never enough of anything because the Americans were over here.

'Mum and Dad depended entirely on the newspaper, and later our radio, for news about the war, and I can remember my parents sitting at the breakfast table on the farm. Dad was very concerned about the advance of the Japanese in the Pacific. He felt we were very vulnerable. When we saw a photo in the newspaper of the American forces marching down Queen Street in Brisbane, he said, "That will be one of the best sights we'll ever see". Mum agreed.'

The support for American servicemen was demonstrated in April 1941 when people from Palmwoods lined the road as visiting sailors travelled up the Montville road and paid a visit to Palmwoods State School. The *Nambour Chronicle and North Coast Advertiser* reported that two children gave welcome speeches at the function, '... Master Ivan Harrison, speaking on behalf of the boys and Miss Pixie Annat, for the girls.' The article continued: 'With all the assurance and aplomb of seasoned speakers, these two gifted speakers conveyed messages that went right to the hearts of those whom they were delighted to honour ... In unfaltering tones, Pixie Annat said ... "We take off our hats to your really great leader, President Franklin Roosevelt. (Cheers). Our hearts throb with gratitude at the help he is giving our Empire in her hour of need. May the Union Jack and Old Glory proudly float for all time as emblems of freedom and liberty".'

Queensland, and in particular Brisbane, became an important base for the Americans during the war in the Pacific. At the peak of the war, there were almost 80,000 US military personnel in Brisbane.

The state's vulnerability to Japanese invasion was underlined by the torpedoing by a Japanese submarine of an Australian hospital ship, the *Centaur*, on 14 May 1943 off Stradbroke Island, not far from the Sunshine Coast. Of the 332 people on board, 268, including 11 nurses, died when the ship was sunk. Australians, including Pixie's parents, were deeply upset by the tragedy of the *Centaur*, and later, when they moved to Brisbane, the Annat family became deeply involved with the Centaur Memorial Fund Committee in honour of the nurses who died. Work with the Centaur Memorial Fund was to become a lifelong commitment for Pixie.

During the final years of the war, however, the focus was on defending Brisbane and the Queensland coast from attack, with the area's maritime defences stretching from the Sunshine Coast to Fort Lytton near Wynnum. Defences included gun emplacements, command and battery observation posts, barbed-wire entanglements on the beaches, tank traps embedded in the sand, and a submarine boom across the shipping channel at the mouth of the Brisbane River.

Volunteers played an important part in planning the defence of Brisbane and surrounding towns, and Jim and Madoline wanted to make a contribution to the war effort. Jim tried to join the local volunteer defence corps (VDC), led by Frank Nicklin – but he was rejected because of the leg injury he had suffered during World War I: 'He came home and said, "They won't even let me join the VDC".' Local defence corps parades were held on Wednesday evenings and Saturday afternoons, and one of the main duties was to guard the beaches from Noosa to Caloundra – viewed as potential landing places for Japanese ships. The defence corps also guarded main roads and railway bridges, and they reported every plane that passed overhead to the Allied headquarters in Brisbane. In Palmwoods, Madoline headed the local first-aid post.

During this time, the Memorial Hall continued to serve as an important meeting place and rallying point for the local community. Everyone played their part, and so it was in March 1942 that Pixie and Ellie were part of a Palmwoods matinee concert arranged by their mother and other members of the local Women's Auxiliary. It would have been a long afternoon for a patient audience, with dozens of children performing. The twins sang a duet, 'There's a Boy Coming Home on Leave', and were in the chorus of the song, 'The Wedding of the Painted Doll'. Pixie recalled that on this occasion it was her sister who did most of the singing: 'She had a lovely voice while I couldn't sing a note, and I heard an army officer in the front row of the audience comment, "Who said she could sing?"'

The twins also participated in the annual children's fancy dress ball, and in November 1942 Pixie and her friend Irene Meder had the honour of handing a cheque to Frank Nicklin for 'convalescing sick and wounded soldiers, sailors and airmen' who had returned from the battlefront.

In 1944, Pixie and Ellie were 15 years old and attending Nambour State High School when they were given the joyful news that their brother had returned safely to England. At the time they were boarding in a private home and shared a large bedroom with another young boarder, Val Alcorn. The house was high up near the hospital and their bedroom had big bay windows: 'Sometimes before the blackouts started, we would just sit and stare out of the windows at the street lights. We'd never seen street lights before, living on the farm, so we thought this was marvellous.'

The twins completed their Junior Commercial Certificates in 1945, and the girls once again excelled academically. Their father was keen for them to complete 'senior', a rare privilege afforded to few pupils in those days. But in the end, they both left school at the end of that year because their mother was determined to sell the farm and move to Brisbane.

'What really finished us at Palmwoods was that the farmers had been promised, by City Electric Light, known as CEL, that electricity was coming from Nambour. The electricity was supposed to come up the Palmwoods–Montville Road where all the farms were, but for some reason it was decided to take electricity out through Hunchy, which was the land between Palmwoods and the Blackall Range. We were told to get ready for electricity by putting up a power pole. We got our power pole and we waited and waited, and then Mum and Dad got a notice to say the electricity supplier was going out to Hunchy.

'Mum said to Dad, "I'm going to Nambour to ask them to sell the farm. I'm not staying here anymore without electricity". So Mum went to see the agent, Jimmy Grimes, in Nambour and told him, "We're selling the farm".'

The sale of the farm was concluded very quickly, and in January 1946 the family camped at Cotton Tree, Maroochydore – camping was a common way to holiday in those days. It was a brief, happy interlude until their permanent move from the coast to Brisbane.

For the first few months in Brisbane they lived with Madoline's brother, Eric Chambers, and his family in Alderley while Jim began the hunt for a house of their own. While the problem of finding a home and a livelihood in Brisbane occupied their parents' minds, Pixie and Ellie were only too pleased to start a new chapter in their lives. Ellie said, 'We were pleased to be off the farm. I vowed that I would never milk a cow or eat porridge again and I never did.'

## Chapter 2

# A Fair Go for Nurses

## 1946–1953

VE Day (Victory in Europe) on 8 May 1945 signified the end of the war in Europe, and the Annats, like all Australians, were hopeful that soon the war in the Pacific would be over, too. So there was great celebration on 15 August on VP Day (Victory in the Pacific) when the news spread that the war had ended. In Brisbane, crowds converged in Queen Street when Prime Minister Ben Chifley announced on the radio that Japan had surrendered.

The euphoria quickly gave way to widespread anxiety – a massive job lay ahead to rebuild the economy that for six years had been directed to meeting the requirements of war. A shortage of housing was a huge problem and rationing of basic goods was still in place. While the departure of American troops was generally not lamented by people in Brisbane, Jim and Madoline Annat would always believe that Australia owed a huge debt of gratitude to General Douglas MacArthur and his troops who had called Australia, and Brisbane, home for about four years.

After the war, Don moved to Sydney briefly to study at the Marconi School of Wireless – the institution where thousands of people had learnt wireless communication skills so vital on ships and aircraft in the two world wars. His early career became a lifelong passion, and Don later became the senior air traffic controller for Queensland.

The immediate problem facing Jim and Madoline was to secure a house for the family – permits were needed to rent or buy a house, part of a complex system devised by the Housing Commission to try to regulate the overtaxed system.

'Dad stayed for a short time with his mother in Buranda while he looked for a house. He came home one night and his mother said, "Well, did you get a house?" Dad said, "Yes, I bought a shop – it was the only way I could get somewhere for us to live".

'Dad bought a corner shop opposite the Wilston Station. It had a two-bedroom house at the back of the shop with the toilet in the back yard. My mother said, "But we don't know anything about shops". Dad said, "Well, we'll learn. We've got to have somewhere to lay our heads". And they made a marvellous business out of that shop, but they worked like devils – my mother always said it was worse than the dairy farm.

'So Mum and Dad ran the corner store and all four of us lived at the back. Ellie and I used to help in the shop on weekends when there was still rationing in place. People often came down to try to get butter, tea and sugar and all sorts of things without coupons, and of course we couldn't sell anything without them. Everything was in short supply. Tobacco wasn't rationed, but it was just not available so people used to try to talk us into selling them more than one packet of cigarettes if we had any.'

After two years the family sold the shop and bought a house in the nearby suburb of Windsor, just a few kilometres from the Brisbane General Hospital. By then the twins had office jobs, having studied Pitman shorthand and typing as part of the Junior Commercial Certificate they attained at Nambour State High School. Pixie was not a shorthand typist for very long, but her shorthand skill was extremely useful and she used it throughout her working life. Her decision to become a nurse was a gradual one. Of the sisters, Ellie had expressed the greater interest in nursing, but she found a typing job with T&G Insurance Company. Pixie was employed in the Brisbane General Hospital board office, meeting often with Eunice Enright, who was secretary to Matron Christense Sorensen.

'I had quite a lot to do with the nursing staff because my job involved rationing and taxation. Working as a typist was terribly repetitive and one day I asked myself "What am I doing here?" My friend Marge Shaw, who worked on the switchboard, had asked me to get her a training application form from Eunice. So in early 1948, I asked Eunice for two application forms, one for Marge and one for me.

'Eunice said to me, "I can imagine Marge as a nurse but never you". And I thought, "Blow you!" We both filled out the forms – Marge lasted three weeks as a trainee nurse. In those days applicants weren't properly interviewed.

Years later, in 1967, I was with my mother in the recreation room of the Lady Lamington Nurses' Home at the hospital, for the Royal Children's Hospital's centenary celebrations. At the time, my mother was secretary of the Royal Brisbane Hospital nurses' club and I was there in my capacity as matron of St Andrew's War Memorial Hospital. Eunice was there, too; she had been living in Africa and was back in Brisbane visiting family. She came up to me and said, "Excuse me, Pixie Annat, what did you do with yourself?" I told her I was matron at St Andrew's – she was dumbfounded, and I reminded her "you could never imagine me as a nurse".'

Through good fortune, Jim Annat also secured work at the Brisbane General Hospital. The accountant, Mr Peachey, had mentioned to Pixie that there was a job going in the pay office. By then Jim was working for his brother-in-law – his sister, Helen, was married to Ernie Silverton, who owned a general store in the suburb of Newmarket.

'It was just before I finished working at the board office, I went home and said to Dad, "There's a job going in the pay office, and Mr Peachey asked if you would apply for an interview". Dad was very reluctant, saying he felt he was unqualified. But I insisted that he was good with figures. So he dressed in his best suit for the interview and that night he came and told us, "I got the bloody job!" He was there for 13 years. For many years afterwards, people would mention that they remembered my father. He enjoyed a friendly chat and joke with nurses and other staff on payday, and he loved talking to them all. I think they were 13 of the happiest years of his life.'

Throughout her training at the Brisbane General Hospital, Pixie would usually spend her days off duty at her parents' home in Windsor, and she remained very involved with her family – she and Ellie were still close and shared many interests.

Both sisters had joined the Centaur Younger Set, and were dedicated members of the Centaur choir. The Centaur Memorial Fund was a big interest for Pixie later in her life; but even as young women, she and Ellie were enthusiastic fundraisers for Centaur. In 1948, the fund was raising money to buy a building dedicated to nurses in memory of those who had died on the *Centaur*. The fund was championed by the editor of the *Brisbane Telegraph*, AR Vickers, and attracted widespread public support, enough to raise £80,000, enabling the purchase of Centaur House in Queen Street, which became the centre for the nursing profession for almost 25 years. The opening of Centaur House in 1949 was a big occasion in Brisbane, and the first person to sleep at Centaur House was the sole nurse survivor of the *Centaur* sinking, Sister Ellen Savage.

'I spoke to her on the night they opened Centaur House and said, "Just as well you were the champion schoolgirl swimmer of New South Wales or you wouldn't have lasted too long". She told me the story of how she went down with all the other girls when the ship was struck, but there was a second explosion and she was literally blown up to the top. It was just dawn and she could see some people on a raft of sorts. She swam towards them and one of the men who had also survived put out his hand to pull her out of the water. He said, "Over here, Sister". She was naked because all her clothes had been blown off. So this fellow took off his shirt and wrapped it around her. She stayed on the water for 38 hours tending to the survivors. She was later awarded a medal for bravery. It was a great privilege to know her.'

Centaur House was officially opened just a few months after Pixie had commenced training at the Brisbane General Hospital. The General Hospital, later called the Royal Brisbane Hospital, was Pixie's workplace for almost 15 years, and it came to have a special place in her heart. The hospital had a rich though somewhat fraught early history. It opened in 1867 on Bowen Bridge Road in Herston, on the site of the 'quarries', and was initially managed by a voluntary committee. In 1917, shortly after Madoline Annat began her training, the Queensland government took control of the hospital in the face of its floundering financial position. By the time Pixie started working at the hospital, the vast site was already the largest hospital complex in Australia, consisting of many separate wards and buildings, treating general patients, and with a separate Children's Hospital and Women's Hospital.

Pixie commenced training as a first-year nurse shortly after the Queensland Labor government introduced free hospital care. This led to a huge increase in patient numbers – by 1946, the 1,000-bed hospital had more than 1,300 daily inpatients, and at the same time the hospital was experiencing a nursing shortage, due in large part to pitifully low nurses' wages. The pay of a first-year nurse in 1948 was one pound, four shillings and nine pence a week – even 16-year-old shop assistants earned more money. Nurses were also provided board, which was considered part of their wages.

In the mid-20th century, nursing at the Brisbane General Hospital was based on the Nightingale nursing and hospital system, which was the accepted method in Australia and in many other countries. It was an arrangement that had brought great improvements for patients, but it also created an authoritarian nursing culture, similar to a military environment, that reflected a generally conservative attitude to life. The pavilion principle, introduced by Florence

Nightingale, where large open wards were devoted to treating specific illnesses, had been incorporated into the early design of the hospital. This included the original Wattlebrae Infectious Diseases Hospital, built in 1911, which had four open-air pavilions where patients were nursed on verandahs, with a small central brick building for some conditions. The building also housed the famous Sister Kenny Baths, where polio patients were treated. Wattlebrae was a facility Pixie would come to know very well indeed.

From its earliest days, nursing at the hospital operated in a highly ordered, hierarchical way – the general medical superintendent and other doctors were seldom challenged by nurses, and nurses themselves were very strictly managed, with the general matron held in great awe. Nurse training at the hospital was based on a traditional apprenticeship model: those in their first three months of training were probationers, and trainees were graded by year level, with caps for different years depicting their status as trainees. Fourth years wore small tulle veils. After four years of training, nurses progressed to wearing white veils when they were granted registration as staff nurses. Next in the hierarchy came charge nurses, who were the 'work horses' of the hospital, and then block sisters who were responsible for supervising a block of the hospital.

All trainees lived at the Lady Lamington Nurses' Home, which by the 1950s consisted of two four-storey wings and the original two-storey building. There was a recreation room, small 'cubicle' bedrooms and shared bathrooms. A strict curfew of 10.30 pm applied, except for Saturdays when this was extended to 12.15 am, and every night the home matron would do her rounds to ensure all the nurses were in bed.

Pixie, like her mother before her, cared for patients in the large wards at the Brisbane General Hospital, with screens the only privacy for these sick people. Nursing duties included linen sorting and making beds, making bandages, sterilising equipment, sharpening needles, and cleaning and caring for patients. Tedious counting of medical devices like thermometers, as well as accounting for all crockery and cutlery, was a much-loathed task that had to be completed at the end of a long shift. There was a very particular pecking order in assigning work; junior nurses, for example, were required to clean the pan room, and pans were expected to shine like mirrors. The first junior on a ward in the morning had to take all the patients' temperatures. Nurses commonly worked 12-hour shifts, with the morning shift starting at 6.00 am and ending at 6.00 pm. On commencing duty, nurses would sponge bath patients, change beds, receive and serve meals, all before the doctors arrived for their morning rounds.

Pixie was reasonably well prepared for what life would be like as a nurse, thanks to her mother's stories and because her aunt Nel Chambers, her mother's sister, had also trained at Brisbane General Hospital. Excited and eager to learn, Pixie began her training in late 1948, spending her first three weeks in the preliminary school based at the hospital, where the young probationers received basic nurse training and were prepared for the busy days that lay ahead. The trainee nurses were assigned to a specific ward for 12 weeks, such as casualty, surgical, medical, children's, psychiatric or geriatric, or to the operating theatres. The tutor sisters, many of whom were ex-army nurses, were highly regarded – and their expertise made up for the rather dated formal curriculum. The students attended all lectures in their own time in the training school.

'The student nurses had to tell the charge nurse of the ward of their lecture timetable for the following week so the rosters could be adjusted to fit this in. So if you started a shift at 6.00 am, you often worked till 9.30 am and went to lectures from mid-morning until lunchtime. Then you returned to duty at 4.30 pm and worked until 9.30 pm. We hated those particular split shifts.'

The Lady Lamington Nurses' Home, which was 'up the hill' from the hospital, was the mainstay of Pixie's life for the next five years. Routine and discipline were emphasised. The student nurses had to rise before dawn, wash, dress, go on duty for 6.00 am, do ward duties, rush to breakfast (which was served in the hospital dining room), go back to their rooms to make their beds, and then hurry down to the hospital to continue their morning shifts. The evening shift began at 6.00 pm, the night shift at 10.00 pm, and after years of working many night shifts Pixie would come to dislike the early nightfall of Brisbane in winter – 'where you began and ended your working day in the dark'.

While the standard of training provided to the young nurses in the late 1940s and early 1950s at the hospital's training school was good thanks to the tutors and ward sisters, the curriculum had not changed substantially for many decades. Looking back at those times, it is abundantly clear that nurses were undervalued and poorly paid. Nurses were caught in a slow-to-change social and health system that had taken root during the early decades of the 20th century. From the 1950s, a gradual but committed battle began to change the way nurses were treated and educated, with nursing leaders like Pixie determined that nurses be seen not as a cheap labour pool but as students and graduates of an important profession.

When Pixie began at the Brisbane General Hospital, nurses were required to complete four years of training, overseen by the Nurses' Registration

Board and the Australasian Trained Nurses' Association (ATNA). Since the Australasian Trained Nurses' Association also represented nurses, those who led the organisation were frequently trying to balance competing interests.

Among the perennial issues that nursing organisations debated for years were training, working conditions and nursing duties. In the 1920s, for example, the Australasian Trained Nurses' Association opposed a campaign to reduce weekly working hours from 56 to 48, claiming that a reduction in hours would impact on education and on patients. There were numerous occasions in the years ahead when organisations representing nurses or nurse administrators battled it out on behalf of their members, and they sometimes clashed with one another.

In the 1940s, the Australasian Trained Nurses' Association in Queensland – which later adopted the name the Royal Australian Nursing Federation Queensland Branch – supported an initiative to form the College of Nursing Australia for postgraduate training. The creation of the college was an important development for nurse education, yet it added to the complexity of issues that nursing organisations were expected to manage. It was also a time when nurses, particularly younger women, were becoming more vocal about their wages and working conditions.

In 1946, the Australasian Trained Nurses' Association failed in a submission to the Queensland Industrial Court for an increase in nurses' wages, much to the disappointment of nurses at the Brisbane General Hospital. At the time, there was uneasiness about a 'trade union' role for the nurse body. The first nurse to become president of the Queensland branch of the Australasian Trained Nurses' Association, Eunice Paten, disliked trade unionism, yet always professed that the organisation was committed to improving conditions for nurses. This same dilemma would later challenge Pixie in her many senior roles with the Royal Australian Nursing Federation (RANF).

Younger student nurses began to express a determination to have their voices heard, and in 1951 a Student Nurses Unit (SNU) was established at the Brisbane General Hospital with Pixie elected its first president. While the new student body was affiliated with the RANF, the charge sisters – who were the senior nurses at the hospital – did not approve of this new association. The SNU was nevertheless popular with student nurses at many Queensland hospitals. According to Pixie, it was the SNU at the Brisbane General Hospital that successfully pushed for the creation of a new committee representing students, all levels of registered nurses and some medical practitioners, to give input into the overall administration of clinical areas.

'I guess what really got to me was injustice. I felt the student nurses weren't always getting a fair go, and that's why I got involved.'

Many nurses of this era, while in hindsight critical of the draconian rules and regulations that governed nurses' lives, were nevertheless proud of their service and made close, lifelong friendships working in the demanding wards and operating theatres and living in the Lady Lamington Nurses' Home. Well into her 80s, Pixie still kept in touch with the friends she made while working at the Royal. And at the time, as a young woman, the low pay, hard work and low status as a junior nurse did not stop her from pursuing her profession. She thrived as a nurse from the outset.

'Because I had worked in the hospital for two years before I started nursing, I wasn't in fear of it in any way. I loved it, absolutely loved it. I liked being able to feel that I was helping someone who was very sick, hearing a patient who would say, "Oh, I do feel so comfortable now".'

Pixie's simple expression of satisfaction in caring for patients was not a platitude – from her earliest days as a junior nurse and right through her senior nursing career, this was always at the heart of what she practised, to make sure patients were not only getting good medical treatment but genuine care as well. However, getting things done properly, in Pixie's opinion, meant doing things efficiently. Her friends – nursing colleagues and doctors – well remember the young nurse Pixie who always worked on the double, getting tasks done competently.

Pixie's years as a young nurse were also greatly shaped by the big health challenges of the time, such as tuberculosis (TB), the leading cause of death from a notifiable disease in the early 1950s. The old Diamantina Hospital at South Brisbane, which had been neglected for many years, was managed by the Brisbane and South Coast Hospitals Board, which also ran the Brisbane General Hospital. Student nurses were required to spend six months of their training at the Diamantina Hospital, caring for TB and geriatric patients.

'I really realised that nurses weren't getting a fair go when we were sent to the Diamantina Hospital – this was later where the Princess Alexandra Hospital was built. It was a terrible place in those days. Our stay at the hospital was referred to as "doing time at the Diam".'

And so, in 1949, at a time when the Brisbane coal strikes were in progress, Pixie and scores of her young nursing colleagues moved from the Lady Lamington Nurses' Home into grim old huts on the South Brisbane Auxiliary Hospital site to commence their rotation.

'It was dreadful. We lived in huts similar to those the airmen had been housed in during the war. There were cracks in the floor and it was freezing cold – there was no hot water, thanks to the coal strikes. For six months, we did not have a hot bath; we would boil kettles and bathe standing up.'

The nurses had a long list of complaints, including the absence of blinds in the night quarters that made it difficult to sleep on hot, sunny days. Another grievance was a very loud hooter that was periodically sounded throughout the day in the engineers' area close to the night quarters.

'We were all in the same boat, but we felt some things could easily be improved. So 30 of us decided to go and see the matron of the Diamantina Hospital, Miss Coker. We went down to see her, three abreast, ten deep, at 9.00 am. From her door, Matron could see my friend, Val Purcell. She said, "Come in, Nurse" and 30 of us walked into her office. Val, June Young and I were the representatives – we said our piece and we tried to be reasonable about it. We wanted her to know we had the support of the other nurses on night shift, all except for one nurse who thought we shouldn't be complaining. Matron Coker was very unreceptive, and as we walked out she said, "I am going to let Matron Sorensen know about this". Miss Sorensen was the general matron of the Brisbane General Hospital, and she was thinking Miss Sorensen would chastise us for this. I turned around and said, "I hope you do".'

Matron Sorensen certainly did hear about this unprecedented protest, and a visit of the facility was arranged for Miss Sorensen and Dr Aubrey Pye, who was the general medical superintendent at the Brisbane General Hospital. Pixie would not have the satisfaction of witnessing this long-awaited inspection because of the rule that if a nurse's family lived in Brisbane, they were not permitted to remain in nurses' quarters at the Diamantina on their days off. Pixie's day off coincided with the visit, and she had to return to her parents' home in Windsor on the day of the inspection. But she was regaled afterwards with the account of this little triumph.

'One of the things that we had complained about was the hooter in the engineers' area. The general medical superintendent of Diamantina, Dr Karl Uhd, was escorting Dr Pye. He assured Dr Pye that our complaint about the noise was a load of rubbish. They had done their rounds and were going down the stairs, and suddenly the hooter went off. Dr Pye got such a fright he slipped down two stairs. He looked at Dr Uhd, who was at the bottom of the stairs, and said, "Turn that bloody thing off! I couldn't sleep with that either!" That was reported to me with great gusto the next day when I got back. The blinds went up, the hooter went off and other small changes were made. So I was satisfied and pleased that it had happened.'

At Diamantina, TB patients were accommodated in the open-air pavilions, with blinds rolled down when needed. Pixie recalled a rather strange case during her time there: 'One night, the night sister and I had just done a round. There were several Aboriginal male patients, most of whom were jockeys who had contracted TB. One of these patients was very anxious, so I offered to make him a cup of tea. When I came back with the tea, a man in the bed opposite said, "Too late, Nurse. He's gone. The man in the bed next to him pointed the bone at him". He had actually died while I was away making the tea. I rang the night sister and told her what had happened. She told me that this was no joking matter, and I said I wasn't joking. So we got the doctor, and the death certificate said: "Bone pointed at man who died of fright".'

Another notifiable disease that was greatly feared was polio (poliomyelitis or infantile paralysis), with epidemics occurring in Australia in the 1930s, 1940s and 1950s at intervals of three to five years. By 1948, concern was once again growing in Queensland about the possibility of a new outbreak of infantile paralysis. The Director-General of Health in Queensland, Dr Abraham Fryberg, had reassured the public that accommodation and staff were available at the Brisbane General Hospital to deal with isolated cases, saying that a new epidemic was not expected before 1949. In reality, the Brisbane General Hospital was groaning with patients of all types, with every ward filled to overflowing. Doctors had long lists of patients to treat, and they would do morning rounds accompanied by sisters and nurses who followed the doctors' instructions.

One section of the hospital that the doctors and nurses came to know very well was the Wattlebrae Infectious Diseases Hospital open-air pavilions, and later a new Wattlebrae ward. Starting in late 1948, Pixie spent six months nursing polio patients at Wattlebrae.

'We went through some pretty terrible times. Polio patients were placed in iron lungs to help them breathe. We had to take them out gradually as they regained the ability and confidence to breathe on their own. I had one young woman patient who told me she had four young children and a violent husband. One morning I told her I would begin her rehabilitation by taking her out for an hour a day, and I told her I would stay with her the whole time. She looked at me and said, "You know, Nurse, if I get out of here I've got to go home and make puddin's [dinner] for the kids". I didn't know what to say. She died the next week. I often wondered what happened to her children.'

At that time, nurses at the Brisbane General Hospital were very interested and proud of the legendary Sister Elizabeth Kenny, the New South Wales nurse who had served on Allied ships during World War I, and who pioneered an unorthodox remedial exercise treatment for polio patients. Sister Kenny was a controversial figure, with many doctors opposed to her approach to treating polio and her strongly expressed opinions. But having worked at the Brisbane General Hospital in the 1930s, Sister Kenny was greatly admired by many nurses and medical practitioners.

'Sister Kenny was the subject of a very unfair commission of enquiry, but her method of treatment was ultimately vindicated, much to the annoyance of many doctors of that era.'

Perhaps the most heartbreaking work for the clinical staff was with the many babies and young children who were admitted with whooping cough.

'That was terrible, the worst thing I was ever involved with. Babies up to six months old weren't supposed to get infectious diseases, or that was the wisdom at the time. We simply did not have the drugs to prevent and treat whooping cough. They would cough and you couldn't do a thing for them except hold them, and one just died in my arms. It was heartbreaking work and impossible to console their mothers.'

Whooping cough patients were confined to the isolation ward. They arrived via the casualty department, along with a seemingly endless stream of general patients who always first came to casualty, the department that often seemed close to breaking point. In 1947, a temporary casualty department had been built between two of the main hospital blocks, and this 'temporary arrangement' endured for decades. Under the direction of a registrar, young medical residents, mostly in their second year, ran services from this rudimentary casualty department. The single-storey building consisted of a large central area and ten cubicles where individual patients were examined. With the introduction of free health care in 1948, hundreds of people flocked to 'Cas' every day, where they were either treated as outpatients or admitted to the hospital.

Colleagues who worked with Pixie during this time recall her as a bundle of energy, ever enthusiastic. Every day was filled with dramas – accident victims, people afflicted with serious diseases and others with minor complaints were directed to the various areas of casualty, where they were seen by the residents and nurses. In spite of the difficulties, Pixie felt that the doctors and nurses worked well as a team. Tales that endure are some of the funny moments, such as the day when young Dr Graham Cavaye, after seeing an outpatient, gave Pixie a signed treatment card that said, 'P.S.B.E.O.A.R.P.T.M.'. Pixie was nonplussed and took the note to the supervising sister, who immediately saw this was 'absolute nonsense'. The note was short for: 'Please syringe both ears out and return patient to me'. The sister took a dim view of the joke and reported the matter to the general medical superintendent, Dr Pye. For years to come, somewhat jokingly, Dr Cavaye would remind Pixie that she had 'got him into trouble'.

By the mid-1950s, the introduction of penicillin, as well as the widespread distribution of vaccinations for diseases like polio, brought about dramatic improvements to patient care across Australia, and these advances were naturally felt at the Royal Brisbane Hospital (RBH). While health improvements occurred fairly rapidly, better conditions for nurses lagged far behind. During her training, Pixie gradually became known among her peers as someone who was unafraid to speak up, and this was particularly the case after she became president of the Student Nurses Unit.

'In 1951, I was elected president and Helen Banff, who later became matron at The Wesley Hospital, was treasurer. The matron would often send for me if there was trouble with the nurses.' The matron by this time was Adelaide Billing, who had succeeded Christense Sorensen in January 1952. She assumed this role at a time when there was immense pressure on the overcrowded hospital and ongoing disagreement between the Department of Health, the Australasian Trained Nurses' Association and the Nurses' Registration Board about the direction nurse training should take. Caught in the middle of competing demands and under great work and budget pressures, Miss Billing did her best. But she was a quiet rather than assertive matron, and not as visible around the hospital as her predecessor – most nurses who did not know her well saw her as a remote figure of authority.

Pixie, while always respectful towards Matron Billing, was not quite so in awe of a woman she recalled as having beautiful, auburn curls.

'Adelaide Billing was the daughter of a Methodist minister, and she had trained with my mother. I can remember my mother, who had a wicked sense of humour, saying to me, "Adelaide was the only one of the nurses in my year whom we didn't have anything on!" Later, I realised Adelaide Billing was trying to support the staff in her way. She had a difficult job to do.'

Matron Billing was very interested in improvements that were occurring at other Australian hospitals. After a study tour in 1952, she presented a report to the general medical superintendent, Dr Pye, recommending changes to nurse

Lieutenant James Whamond Annat, Pixie's grandfather, in 1900.

**ABOVE:** Pixie's mother, Madoline Chambers, at the Brisbane General Hospital, 1920.

**RIGHT:** Enoggera Army Barracks, 1915. Pixie's father, James (Jim) Annat, is on the right.

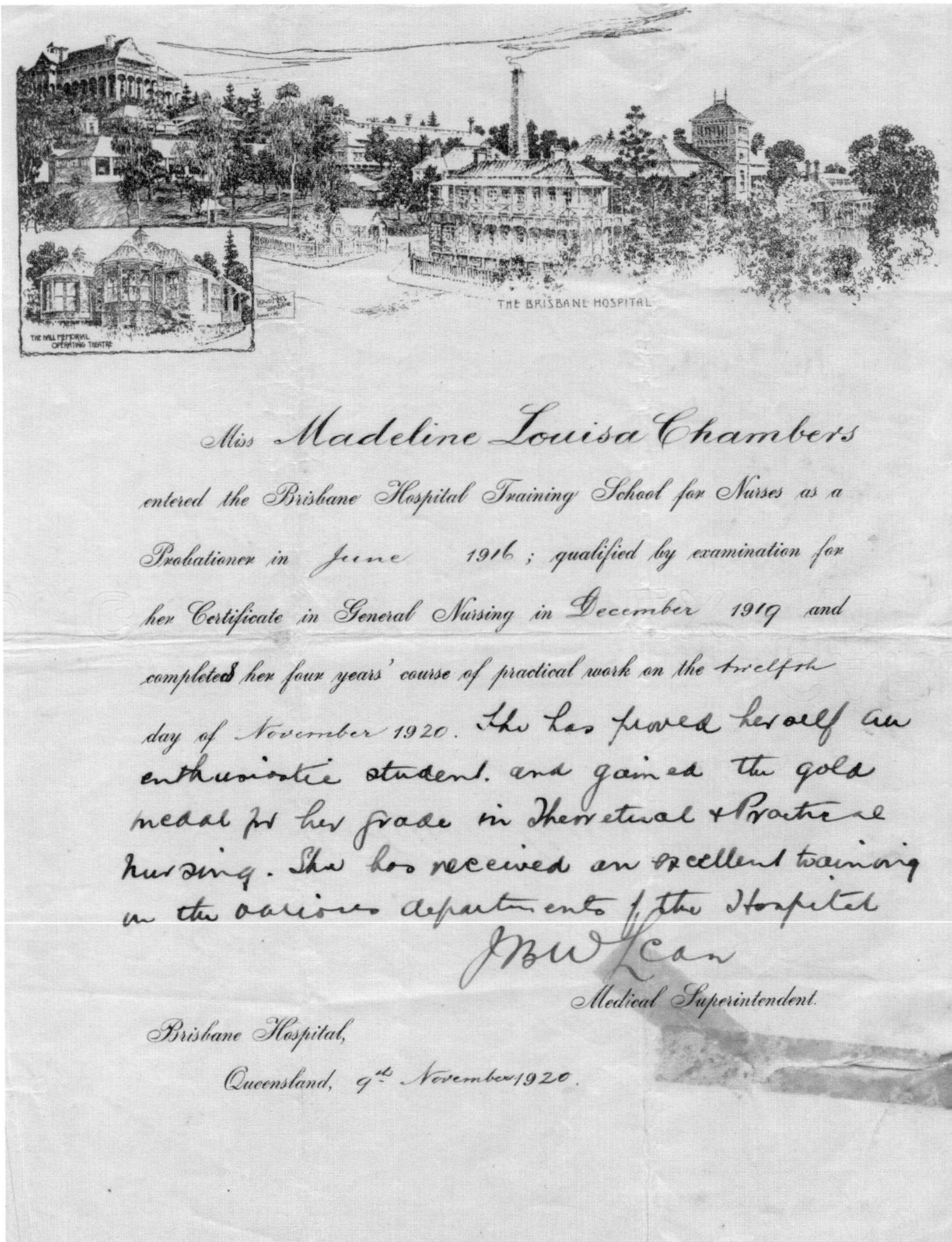



Miss Madeline Louisa Chambers

entered the Brisbane Hospital Training School for Nurses as a Probationer in June 1916; qualified by examination for her Certificate in General Nursing in December 1919 and completed her four years' course of practical work on the twelfth day of November 1920. She has proved herself an enthusiastic student and gained the gold medal for her grade in Theoretical & Practical Nursing. She has received an excellent training in the various departments of the Hospital

JBW Lean

Medical Superintendent.

Brisbane Hospital,

Queensland, 9th November 1920.

Madoline Chambers' (Gold Medalist) Certificate in General Nursing, 1920.

**ABOVE:** Pixie's parents, Madoline and Jim (centre), on their wedding day in Brisbane, 1921. The best man was Harry Bayard and the bridesmaid was Nel Chambers, Madoline's sister.

**RIGHT:** Donald, Pixie and Ellie's brother, at their grandparents' farm near Crow's Nest, Queensland, 1930.

RIGHT: The Annat girls at Palmwoods State School, 1935. Pixie (fifth from the right) and Ellie (far right) are both in the second row. Their teacher was Miss Molly Cranny.

BELOW: Pixie's Grade Three progress report, 1937.

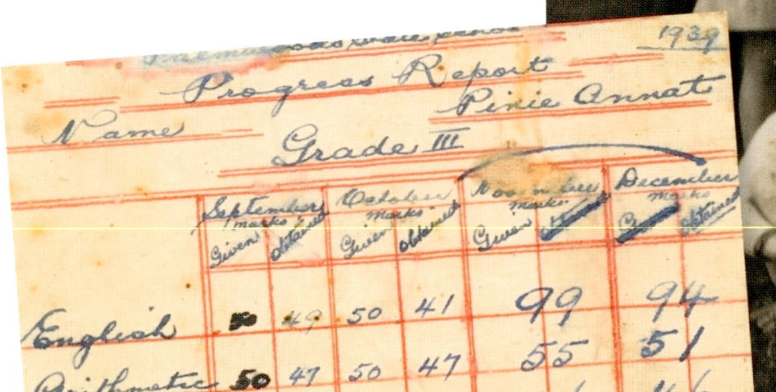

Palmwoods State School 1939

Progress Report

Name Pixie Annat

Grade III

| | September marks Given | September marks Obtained | October marks Given | October marks Obtained | November marks Given | November marks Obtained | December marks Given | December marks Obtained |
|---|---|---|---|---|---|---|---|---|
| English | 50 | 49 | 50 | 41 | 99 | | 94 | |
| Arithmetic | 50 | 47 | 50 | 47 | 55 | | 51 | |
| Other Subjects | 50 | 46 | 50 | 43 | 46 | | 46 | |
| Conduct | 50 | 45 | 50 | 43 | | | | |
| Pad Work | 25 | 25 | 25 | 25 | | | | |
| Attendance | 25 | 25 | 25 | 25 | | | | |
| Home Work | 50 | 50 | 50 | 50 | | | | |
| Percentage | | 95% | | 91% | | | | |
| Teacher's Initials | TSW | | | | | | | |
| Parents Initials | M.L.A. | M.L.A | | | | | | |

Result of Examination 95%.

Place in Class 3.

TSW

PALMWOODS
1935
INFANTS

Don Annat with his squadron in front of their Lancaster bomber in England during World War II.

RIGHT: Don Annat, 1942. He joined the Royal Australian Air Force at 19 years of age.

BELOW: Pixie and Ellie at Surfers' Paradise, Queensland, in 1947.

BELOW RIGHT: Pixie during her first year of nursing training, outside Diamantina Hospital in 1948.

**LEFT:** Pixie and Ellie (first and second from the left) with their dance partners, Ian Taggert and Sonny Grace, at the hospital ball at Cloudland Dance Hall in 1949.

**BELOW:** Don with his first daughter, Leigh, in Cairns, Queensland, in 1949.

**BELOW LEFT:** Pixie and Ellie waiting for a replacement bus after their Sydney-bound tour bus broke down in Tenterfield, New South Wales, in October 1949. It was their first trip outside of Queensland.

TOP: Royal Brisbane Hospital Casualty Department in the late 1940s.

ABOVE: Pixie (front row, second from the left) as a third-year student nurse with day staff at Raff Ward, Royal Children's Hospital, Brisbane, Christmas 1951.

RIGHT: Pixie, in her fourth year of training, on the steps of the Lady Lamington Nurses' Home, Royal Brisbane Hospital, 1952.

The *Esperance Bay* (light-heartedly known as *Desperate Bay* because it was prone to breaking down), 1954. Pixie and Ellie bought this postcard of the ship to remember their voyage to England.

**OPPOSITE PAGE:** Ellie and Pixie at Hamilton Wharf, Brisbane, about to board the *Esperance Bay* bound for London, June 1954.

ABOVE: While living in London in 1954, Ellie (left) and Pixie (third from the left) bought a taxi from the London Taxi Company in Brixton, with their friends, Elaine Locke (far right) and Dell Dunne (second from the left).

LEFT: Pixie and Ellie had learnt to drive as teenagers on their farm, so they were the drivers while Elaine and Dell were chief navigators.

The young Australian women had many adventures in their taxi as they travelled through the English countryside. Here they are in Devon after they'd run out of petrol.

Ellie (far left) and Pixie (third from the left) in Egypt in 1954 on a stopover during their voyage to London.

Pixie at the Pyramids of Giza, Egypt. She's riding the camel on the far right.

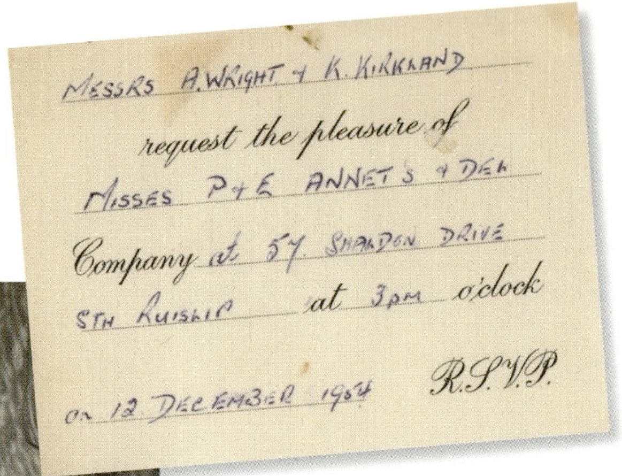
MESSRS A. WRIGHT & K. KIRKLAND
request the pleasure of
MISSES P & E ANNET'S & DEL
Company at 57 SHALDON DRIVE
STH RUISLIP at 3pm o'clock
on 12 DECEMBER 1954 R.S.V.P.

**ABOVE:** While they were living in London in 1954, Ellie and Pixie received this invitation to a reunion of the *Esperance Bay* gang from the young men they had befriended on the ship.

**LEFT:** Last night on the *Esperance Bay*, 25 July 1954: Pixie with Kevin Kirkland (left) and Ellie with Len Stevens.

Kevin and Pixie in 1955 in London.

Ellie and Pixie in sleeping bags while camping in France in 1955.

Pixie and Jimmy Slade at work at Rank's in London, 1955.

training, better organisation of shifts and other ideas to improve the running of the wards. The chief problem, however, was money, and the hospital board resisted changes that would result in reduced staff on the wards. As a result, many of the changes she recommended were slow to occur.

Pixie recalled a day in 1952 when she was once again called into the matron's office:

'One day, when I was in my fourth year, the sister in charge of the ENT theatres, Vi Broadhead, said to me in her very slow way of speaking, "Annat, you're wanted down in Matron's office at three o'clock!" I thought, "Oh no, not again". I put on my little fourth-year veil and trotted down with Helen Banff. I said to her, "It looks like you and I are for the chop". When we got down to Matron's office, there were three other nurses there, Connie McAuley and Joy Lowe and one other. These girls had never put a foot wrong before. We were invited in and I noticed afternoon tea was laid out, complete with Royal Doulton china and sandwiches, and there were five chairs arranged in a semicircle. I assumed that Matron was expecting important guests later. Then she said to Connie, "Nurse, would you pour?" So Connie poured tea for the six of us, and Matron said, "I have called you down because I want your advice". Helen and I could not believe what we were hearing, this was just unheard of. So we discussed her ideas about improving things for student nurses, and we were very supportive of what she was suggesting. Later when I got back to theatre, Broadhead asked me, "Well, Annat, what happened?" I replied, "Actually, we had afternoon tea with Matron". She didn't believe me and told me to get back in theatre on the double.'

'Broadie', as she was affectionately known, left nursing when she got married. (Until 1966, any permanently employed nurse who married forfeited their position in keeping with Queensland public sector employment law.) Pixie lost touch with her until many years later, in the early 1980s, when she was admitted as a patient at St Andrew's War Memorial Hospital.

'I went to see her in the ward and said, "Hello, Broadie!" Before I could say anything, the first thing she asked me was, to my surprise, "Why did you really get called down to see Miss Billing?" I replied, "We went to have afternoon tea with Matron!" She laughed – she thought I had been pulling her leg, because I was always getting into trouble in those days.'

There was a serious side to the work to which Pixie had begun to devote herself, even in these very early days as president of the Student Nurses Unit. In 1951, she flew to Melbourne, her very first flight, to attend the first student nurse conference ever held in Australia, at the Nurses Memorial Centre in St Kilda, where much of the discussion centred on how to build membership of the new student body. Pixie was one of those people who thrived in an environment where there was a lot of discussion. She had the confidence to express her opinions, and she thoroughly enjoyed this, the first of hundreds of conferences and forums she would attend in her many decades of professional and voluntary service.

As a young nurse leader, Pixie was a sponge and she loved meeting new people. So during this, her first visit to Melbourne, she was excited to meet an icon, 'an absolute giant' of Australian nursing.

'On the second day of the conference, the contingent of five nurses from Queensland were told that a Miss Wilson wished to see us. It turned out this was Matron Grace Wilson, one of Australia's best-known nurses from World War I, who had literally constructed the hospital on the island of Lemnos off Gallipoli under most extraordinary conditions.'

Brisbane-born Grace Wilson, who after World War II had senior roles in the Australian Red Cross and in health care in Victoria, was keen to meet the Queensland contingent of young nurses, and on meeting Pixie she invited the five nurses to join her for dinner and a theatre musical the following evening. 'We could not believe our ears. She told us she had a great interest in student nurses. We had a marvellous time, this was just an amazing treat for us.'

Like so many of Pixie's stories, there was an interesting little twist to the tale. During a conversation with Miss Wilson, it transpired that Pixie's father had owned the farm next door to Grace's brother, Roy Wilson, at Victoria Point.

'After the conference when I got home, I said to Dad, "Do you remember Grace Wilson?" He said, "Of course, every soldier on Gallipoli knew Grace Wilson". I said, "Why didn't you tell me about her before?" And I told him about what she had done. He said, "That would be typical of her".'

In October 1952, after sitting their final exams, Pixie and 16 fellow nurses finally completed their four years of training. While Pixie's mother had been the gold medallist in 1919, awards had been discontinued in 1926 and were only reinstated in 1953. Pixie did very well in her exams and was not too concerned about the absence of prizes. At the graduation ceremony, each nurse was presented with a certificate signed by Matron Adelaide Billing certifying that they had successfully completed 'four years of general training at the hospitals governed by the Brisbane and South Coast Hospitals Board'.

In 1953, Pixie decided to undertake her midwifery training at the Maroochy District Hospital in Nambour. This town where she had attended high school still felt like home, and after strenuous years at the RBH, Pixie wanted to get away for a while from the 'big hospital syndrome'. Midwifery was not her particular calling, but she felt that her training would be incomplete without this experience. The Nambour area, just 19 kilometres from the coast, had not changed a great deal since the Annat family's departure from the 'North Coast' following World War II. The Maroochy District Hospital, later named the Nambour General Hospital, had been built in 1930 high on the hill on Hospital Road, and by then was funded by the Maroochy Shire. It occupied an important place in the town, catering for 4,000 or so residents and many other people from the surrounding farms, with both public and private wards available to patients.

The general medical superintendent was Dr Jack Moffat, a highly regarded doctor who trained many young residents in his long career at the hospital: 'Dr Moffat had a terrible stutter, but his medical knowledge was terrific. He used to write everything down, which the nurses loved, because we then had a full account of what had happened with a patient and what he wanted us to do.'

Pixie recalled an occasion when a former nurse from the Nambour General Hospital presented to the labour ward, with the baby breached: 'My friend was on duty this evening in the labour ward and the mother had a pretty torrid time, but all went well and Dr Moffat delivered a healthy baby, much to everyone's relief. My friend told me that Dr Moffat had been so absorbed that he never stuttered once.'

It turns out that Pixie had been wise to choose Nambour General Hospital: 'It was a good hospital to do your "mid" – in the year it took to complete midwifery, most of us helped deliver 50 babies. Down at the Brisbane General Hospital it was much more difficult to get your numbers. Midwives needed 25 deliveries to complete their training, and at Nambour I was very fortunate to gain so much practical experience.

'Of course, I adored all the babies. But there was one little baby in the nursery who had been born prematurely and was very small and thin. This made us love her all the more. Soon after the birth, the father arrived with a few of his friends on motorbikes, all dressed in leathers. These burly bikies wanted to see the new baby through the nursery window. For one second I thought perhaps I should show them another, bigger, baby. But of course I couldn't really do that, so I showed the dad his actual child. This young fellow swung around and said, "Here you are, fellas! Ain't she a whopper?" I will never forget the look on those men's faces as they peered at this tiny baby.'

## Chapter 3

# Innocent Travelling Days

## 1954–1956

By late 1953, Pixie had completed her midwifery training in Nambour and had moved back to Brisbane, to the family home in Windsor. Australia at this time was still closely connected to the British Empire – and so the 1954 royal tour by the newly crowned Queen Elizabeth II and Prince Philip was a huge occasion. In Brisbane, the Queen's visit in March 1954 was greatly anticipated. Most of the Annat family, including Pixie, joined the 40,000 people who lined George Street to witness the Queen's arrival. The excited crowd was thrilled at the spectacle of the royal cavalcade's entrance at City Hall amid the visual display of city buildings festooned with flags and bunting for the royal visit.

'My mother took her own mother, who was in her late 80s at the time, to see the Queen leave Government House. My grandmother was English. As the Queen passed by, she raised her hand and said, "Best wishes, Your Majesty".'

In the 1950s, close bonds between Australia and Britain were strengthened by continued migration – hundreds of thousands of British migrants arrived by ship after the war, with large numbers coming to Queensland every year in the 1950s. Australia at the time had a White Australia Policy, and under this it favoured British migrants, who were known as '£10 Poms' because of the assisted passage they received. There was also great interest in travel by ships bound for Britain, and the big cruise companies like P&O advertised their glamorous-sounding trips to England, which helped fill the migrant vessels on their return journeys from Australia. *The Courier-Mail* regularly featured advertisements for the shipping lines, and in early 1954 Pixie and Ellie pored over them; they were very taken with the Aberdeen Commonwealth Line, which offered travel to England via Colombo, Suez and Malta. The one-way fare was £99. So the sisters, with their friends, Dell Dunn and Elaine Locke, began planning this trip, intending to work in London and tour the United Kingdom and Europe. Their parents supported the travel plans and felt it would be a good opportunity for them to visit England and Scotland, where 'their people' had come from.

The importance of this trip to the Annat family was underlined by the special farewell function for the girls held at Centaur House – the sisters' two-and-a-half years of travelling and living abroad cemented their close bond.

'We were always close because for most of our lives we were always together. When we went to England, Mum said to Dad, "At least they've got each other".'

Their departure from Brisbane on the *Esperance Bay* was delayed by rolling wharf strikes at Australian ports, but they finally set sail on the 32-year-old ship on 1 June 1954. This was one of the last voyages the *Esperance Bay* would make. During the war it had been converted for use as an armed merchant cruiser and later as a troop ship. It was reconditioned after 1945 and used as a cargo and passenger ship until 1955, when it was decommissioned and broken up. There were about 100 passengers on the *Esperance Bay*'s voyage to England, and the girls from Brisbane 'loved every minute' of the experience of being at sea for eight weeks. They enjoyed meeting new people, particularly a group of young men from Australia with whom they became friendly; they continued to see the men in London.

According to Ellie, 'There was a place on the ship called the sun deck. There was a group of us, and the lads called it "the sun deck by day and the sin deck by night … if you're lucky", but that sort of thing didn't happen in those days.'

Arriving in foreign ports was an eye opener for the sisters, who had seldom travelled beyond Queensland in their 24 years. When the *Esperance Bay* docked at Port Said, north of the Suez Canal, they were amazed at the sights and smells and the vast numbers of people. The poverty they saw shocked them. In Aden, before they went up the Suez Canal, they saw entire families – mothers and fathers, children and babies – sleeping in the streets, their few belongings and animals with them. Ellie in particular recalled these scenes as heartbreaking.

Pixie also never forgot sailing into harbour on the island of Malta as the morning sun appeared over the horizon.

'Malta was the headquarters of the British Mediterranean fleet in those days and had been battered during World War II. There were battleships and an aircraft carrier and all these ships lined up. You could sense the power. Our little boat berthed beside all these big ships and unloaded cargo. We were only in Malta for 24 hours, and one of the first things we did was to walk to a church high up on the hill. We spoke to the priest, who pointed to a bomb and cavity in the floor. He told us, "You see that? That bomb landed there during the war and it was never moved, we left it there as a reminder".'

The priest told them that just weeks before their visit, the bomb, which was discovered to be live, had been defused. These reminders of a war now long past always registered with Pixie during her travels in Europe, through England, France, Spain, Sweden, Norway, Italy and Germany – these countries were in various stages of recovery, but the towns, landscape and people still bore the scars and reminders of war.

'I remember in 1955 when Ellie and I were travelling in the north of France by car, we arrived near Ypres and came across a memorial – it was built of steel and was very high. It had "25th Battalion First Australian Imperial Forces" inscribed on it, and that was our dad's battalion. We were standing looking at the memorial when an elderly Frenchman came up to us. We told him our father had been an officer in the 25th Battalion. This old man looked at me, stood to attention and said, "Do you know how tall it is? Exactly ten feet. That is how we saw them".'

When the four Brisbane girls first arrived in London, they found a flat in Kennington, near The Oval Cricket Ground, which they rented for £30 a month. There were two nurses living in the flat above them, and one of them, Margaret Anderson, had been awarded the George Medal for bravery during the evacuation of Singapore. The girls became good friends.

Pixie and Ellie arrived at a time when food rationing had finally come to an end and the city's reconstruction from the Blitz was progressing: 'You could see for miles because of damage – entire areas were still being rebuilt.' It was exciting, glamorous and also quite ugly in parts, and although very different from Brisbane, the girls felt welcomed and at home.

'We loved the tube trains, and the double-decker buses where you could see for miles, and being able to walk past Buckingham Palace and Lambeth Palace – we were Anglicans, and so this was important to us.'

They decided to buy an old taxi from the London Taxi Company to use for touring, and paid £40 for a traditional Austin navy blue taxi that 'resembled a hearse'. Pixie and Ellie got the idea to buy a taxi from several Australians they had met in London who had done the same thing to get around. They parked the old car on the street outside their flat – it had no keys and started with an old-fashioned ignition button. On their many trips around the British Isles, the sisters, who from their farm days were old hands at driving ancient vehicles on narrow roads, were the main drivers while their friends, Dell and Elaine, were the chief navigators.

It was such an unusual undertaking that their exploits in the London taxi were even reported by Australian Associated Press, published in *The Courier-Mail,* with Pixie's mother giving a proud account of her daughters' adventures abroad.

Ellie remembered: 'We'd be driving along and we'd pull up for these hitchhikers, and sometimes they were girls Pixie had trained with at the hospital. So we'd take their bags and put them in the taxi, and head for the youth hostels we were all staying in for the night, it saved them carrying these heavy bags.'

They never had very much money, and as they bumped along through the English countryside, they would frequently call in at farms where they introduced themselves to the farmers and their families; many nights were spent sleeping in the back of the taxi in farmers' fields. They would pull down the back seats and fashion a double bed where all four of them slept.

According to Pixie, 'We stayed on one farm in Wales, and in the morning the farmer came out to see us. We were all up and he looked in the back of the taxi. One of the hens had laid an egg on the back seat. He looked at me, picked up the hen and off he went. Then he turned around and said, "I think you have done this trip in all innocence". And he was dead right. The tyres got so bare we couldn't risk going over cobbles.'

These were very innocent travelling days, and the Australian girls experienced many moments of kindness and hospitality. They travelled to Scotland, where they watched the Edinburgh Tattoo – hearing the lone piper 'made your hair stand on end'. They went to Edinburgh Castle and parked on the side of the road to photograph Balmoral Castle with their box brownie camera.

Ellie fondly recalled: 'A car pulled up in front of us with a Scottish couple in it. They reversed back and said they had noticed the little flag on the corner of the taxi's window. They asked us, "Are you Australians?" We said that we were and that we had stopped to get a photograph of Balmoral Castle. They said, "Come on, we are taking you to lunch". So they took the four of us all through Balmoral Castle Estate and then to lunch. They were Scots and just took a shine to us because we were Australians.'

In London, Pixie and Ellie both found jobs at J Arthur Rank, the English company that produced films, owned cinemas and had diversified into the manufacture of cameras, radios and televisions. Clerks and typists were paid much better wages than nurses, and so Pixie remained with Rank rather than work as a nurse. The sisters worked in different parts of the huge company, and Ellie in particular detested her job in the shipping department. She found a much more suitable position working in the radiology department at St Mary's Hospital in Paddington, but Pixie remained at Rank, where she made many friends.

'We had a very happy social life, I saw a lot of my friend from Sydney, Kevin Kirkland, but he went overland back to Australia, through Asia, before us. He wanted us to travel with him and a friend, but we decided to stay in London.' Pixie, reticent about her personal life, regarded Kevin as 'a very special friend' and sometimes pondered what her life would have been like with him.

By early 1956, Pixie began thinking seriously of returning home – she had no interest in working long-term for Rank. She wanted to resume her nursing career and she persuaded her sister, who was very reluctant to leave London, to go back to Brisbane. They sold their London taxi for £45 – a profit of £5 – and sailed back on the *Orion*. They arrived back in Brisbane as seasoned travellers who could claim that they had seen much of the world.

'During our time abroad, we travelled across most of Europe, camping and staying in youth hostels. We went as far north as almost to the Arctic Circle and as far south as Gibraltar. We were amazed at the hurt that people still felt from the war and the dislike between countries in Europe. The Norwegians we met hated the Swedes; they told us Sweden had let the Germans through. There were these very deep wounds, people were still angry at the shocking things that had happened to ordinary people and this made a big impression on us.'

## Chapter 4

# Sister in Charge

## 1956–1964

Brisbane in 1956 was the proverbial 'big country town', especially compared with the whirl of London. But for Pixie the blue skies and sultry Brisbane weather, and being back with her family and friends, made her feel she was truly home.

She had decided to resume nursing, and now there were new options: in 1956 the Diamantina Hospital had finally been replaced by the new acute-care South Brisbane Hospital – later renamed the Princess Alexandra Hospital. This new hospital was part of a sizeable building program in the 1950s and 1960s, which led to the opening of specialised state hospitals such as the Chermside Chest Hospital (later named The Prince Charles Hospital) and Greenslopes Repatriation Hospital. The state's private hospitals were also being built, such as St Andrew's War Memorial Hospital in 1958, and the Mater Private Hospital was growing. The new South Brisbane Hospital complex included new nursing quarters and more up-to-date hospital facilities, and a number of senior staff and trainees decided to make the move to South Brisbane. Pixie, however, opted to return to the Royal Brisbane Hospital (RBH) as a charge sister, eventually assuming responsibility for the hospital's private patients in the 'intermediate wards' – a job she loved and which she held until 1962.

At this time, there was still a considerable shortage of nurses, not helped by low pay and the strict discipline, including curfews, enforced on live-in trainees. As part of an effort to attract more nurses and improve living conditions, the Lady Lamington Nurses' Home for student nurses was renovated. Living at the hospital was further improved by the construction of a swimming pool in the late 1950s at the rear of Edith Cavell Nurses' Home, where night-duty staff lived. The pool was a very popular spot with nurses during Brisbane's humid summer months. Pixie joined in enthusiastically in social life – her friends from those days describe her as ever-energetic. One of her many interests, which she shared with Ellie, was fencing with the Centaur Fencing Club, and she would often be seen practising her lunges at one end of the recreation room. The 'rec room' was the common area shared by both trainees and registered nurses.

The sisters resumed their involvement in the Centaur Younger Set, which was continuing to raise money for Centaur House in Queen Street. Fundraising events, like cheese and wine nights, theatre nights and dances in the recreation hall at the hospital, absorbed much of their free time.

In 1958, Ellie decided to apply for a job in New Guinea, and it was there she met and married Bruce Murr – in 1961 – and where their son, Peter, was born in 1963. The sisters exchanged letters every week. Pixie also travelled to New Guinea and stayed with her sister for several months in 1963. Every two years, the Murr family visited Brisbane. In these ways, the twins' bond remained strong – and when Ellie and Bruce returned to Brisbane in 1975, Ellie and Pixie picked up where they had left off.

Their brother, Don, after completing his training at the Marconi School of Wireless in Sydney, was appointed as an air traffic controller at the Karumba Flying Boat Base in the Gulf of Carpentaria. In the late 1940s, he moved to Cairns where he met and married Freda Punchard in 1947. They had four children – Leigh, Vicki, Neale and Lawrie who, sadly, died as a baby. The family lived in the Cairns area for many years, and later moved back to Brisbane.

With her brother and sister away from Brisbane for many years, Pixie remained devoted to her parents, returning home regularly, even during the busiest periods of her life. Her new job at the RBH as charge sister of the private wards was a demanding role, and it brought her into contact with many Brisbane specialists, including lifelong friend Dr Sam Mellick, who had graduated with first-class honours from the University of Queensland in 1948. He remembers Pixie as an exacting nurse who gained the respect of doctors. One of her nursing friends at the RBH said that for the most part, nurses were 'petrified' of doctors, but that in spite of this many of the young doctors learnt a great deal from the highly experienced, battle-hardened charge sisters. Pixie by this time was one of these very capable senior sisters. In the private wards, she dealt with doctors, lawyers and 'captains of industry', and, according to her friend, she had a knack for managing them, of getting them 'to eat out of her hands'.

Pixie's view was that the relationship between doctors and senior sisters was usually cordial and friendly, but that if pushed, the experienced sisters could speak up for themselves and their nurses.

'When I was still a trainee, I was in the ward with Sister Mary Dickfos, who was one of the most effective charge nurses at the hospital. That morning, one of the specialists was doing his rounds with Sister Dickfos and he muttered that, "Patients in this hospital get better by good luck, more than by good management". I was following them to carry out Doctor's instructions. The doctor asked for sutures to be removed from one of the patients, and when I went to do this, Sister Dickfos said, "What are you doing, Nurse?" I replied, "I'm going to take the sutures out". Sister said, "Don't worry, Nurse, they'll come out by good luck". So it went on – each time I began to carry out a task the doctor requested, Sister Dickfos would say this wasn't necessary, we should leave it to good luck, until the doctor said, "Oh, all right!" And Sister said to him, "Don't say stupid things, then!" We continued the round, completing all necessary procedures. It was never mentioned again, and the sister and doctor remained great colleagues.

'We worked as a team in those very busy days in casualty, and also in the operating theatres and hospital wards, including in the two wards for private, or "intermediate", patients, which I managed.'

The richness of the stories from those years, from 1956 until 1962 when Pixie was a charge sister, abounds. Another of her anecdotes involved the much-loved general physician Dr Lynn David 'Pappy' Walters. Queensland-born Dr Walters had studied medicine at the University of Sydney in the 1930s – in those days Brisbane did not have a medical school. He then underwent the intense experience of training as a registrar in the Brisbane General Hospital in the 1940s. For years Dr Walters also practised as a consultant physician based at Wickham Terrace in Spring Hill, close to the site of St Andrew's War Memorial Hospital. At many stages during her career, both at the RBH and later at St Andrew's, Pixie worked with Dr Walters, who was renowned for both his practice and teaching of medicine.

'During my time in charge of the private wards at the RBH, Pappy Walters rang me asking whether I had a bed for a Mr Doig, who happened to be the father of Matron Edna Doig, who was principal matron for the Army Northern Command. Mr Doig had been suffering from persistent hiccups for about 24 hours, and Dr Walters had decided to admit him to try to stop the hiccups. Edna arrived to see me – she had come up on the train from Wynnum and told me she had mentioned to a friend she had happened to meet on the train that her father couldn't stop hiccupping. The lady on the train had advised Edna to try the old vinegar remedy, suggesting the patient drink two ounces of pure vinegar without stopping. When Pappy Walters arrived, I told him about this remedy. He decided that the patient should first have an anaesthetic for a short time to try to stop his hiccups. So that was tried, and no sooner had the patient woken up than he started hiccupping again. I gave Dr Walters the news on the phone and he said, "Try the vinegar". So I went in with a cup of pure vinegar and I said, "Now, Mr Doig, I want you to drink this. It's going to be awful, but just swallow it down as though you're drinking a cup of tea". He swallowed it all and I have never seen anyone shudder like that. Within a minute, the hiccups stopped. I rang Pappy Walters and he came in from Wickham Terrace to see the patient. He said, "I find that incredible". He thought the shuddering might have disrupted the irritation of the diaphragm, which occurs with hiccups. Dr Pappy always had a string of students in tow, he was wonderful to work with. He promised to tell his students about this treatment for hiccups.'

This light-hearted story paints only a partial picture of Pixie as a senior nurse. Doctors and nurses who worked with her during those years recall a caring young woman with excellent nursing and organisational skills. She earned the respect of the specialists she worked with, and many were pleased when they encountered her again at St Andrew's War Memorial Hospital several years later.

Pixie's return to the RBH in 1956 rekindled her interest in nursing affairs. The Australasian Trained Nurses' Association Queensland Branch had by then changed its name to the Royal Australian Nursing Federation (RANF) Queensland Branch, and was based at Centaur House. Pixie continued to support the RANF Student Nurses Unit and advocated for improved working conditions and education for nurses.

A major concern, and one that would be expressed time and again, was the low educational standard set for student general nurses, and for many years nursing organisations advocated for the Queensland Junior Public Examination to become the minimum entry standard. There was a high attrition rate among young trainees, many of whom left to get married, and also a high examination failure rate. However, the Queensland government continued to resist calls to raise entry levels, clinging to the old apprenticeship model in order to ensure an adequate labour supply.

Nurse politics in this era, and indeed for decades to come, was complex. There was conflict, for example, in the early 1960s between the RANF and the Matrons Association, a public-hospital-based organisation supported by the Health Minister, with accusations that some of the matrons put loyalty to their employers and medical staff above support for nursing colleagues.

What annoyed many nurses was the attitude of Health Department officials who set the direction of nurse education, including entrance standards and the curriculum, with little regard for the views of nurses themselves. In 1961, a new curriculum supported by the Matrons Association was proposed, but it was not until the following year that the RANF was asked to provide comment. The RANF branded the curriculum poor and outdated, but it was nevertheless approved without raising the entry requirement. Dissatisfaction about the standard of education for nurses would rumble on for many years.

The close relationship between the government and the matrons was evident at the Matrons Association's annual conferences, which were financially supported by the government and routinely opened by the Health Minister. In 1965, after the public announcement that Pixie had been appointed matron at St Andrew's, she was invited to attend the Matrons Association conference 'as a courtesy'. Also in attendance was Director-General of Health Dr Fryberg.

'I met him during the conference and he said to me, "I'm so pleased to see a nice girl like you has gone to St Andrew's". I said, "What are you talking about, Dr Fryberg?" And he said, "Nice girls like you shouldn't be involved in industrial relations". I replied, "I don't know what would happen if we weren't involved". I told him I was particularly concerned where nursing education was headed. He patted me on the arm and said, "You know, Dearie, nurses only have to rub backs and carry pans". And I said, "Well, I hope you are not very sick when you come to hospital, because if that's all they do for you, you will die".'

Pixie had the satisfaction of proving her point to some of her former adversaries when they themselves became patients. In 1959, when she was charge sister at the RBH, one of her patients was an undersecretary from the Health Department, a powerful bureaucrat renowned for being dismissive of nurses. General Medical Superintendent Dr Pye had phoned Pixie to say that this public servant had suffered a serious heart attack, and he instructed her to ensure there was a bed available for him in the intermediate ward.

'I thought to myself, "I can't believe it, this man who I have been arguing with for all these years …" I instructed the nurses to look after him exactly as they would any other very sick patient. He was in the ward for about a month – it was the days before open-heart surgery when the treatment was conservative. Before his discharge I went over his medications and home care with him. He asked me to sit down for five minutes and said, "I owe you an apology. No, I owe the profession an apology. I had no idea what responsibility nurses had. If it hadn't been for you and the staff here, I wouldn't be here." I told him I hoped he would pass that on once he returned to work. The doctors only came in at certain times of the day to see their patients, the rest of the time it was up to you, the nurse. You just did what you had to do for your patients.'

After six years as charge sister of private patients, working ten hours a day, five and a half days a week, Pixie was ready for another challenge. She was also keen to make a difference to policy and left to work full-time for the RANF Queensland, as assistant secretary and then secretary, based at Centaur House. She gained valuable organisational skills in these roles – she travelled regularly across Queensland by aircraft or train, visiting RANF members in the hospitals. By then she had been a longstanding member of the Liberal Party; she counted as one of her big achievements attending a Liberal Party convention in the early 1960s, and moving a motion that was adopted and became government policy, granting superannuation to nurses.

Pixie continued to have a wide group of friends, including a football player boyfriend called Len, but 'I could not see myself spending the rest of my life with him'. Many of her closest friends were nurses or former nurses. One good friend was fellow nurse Fran Ryan, who graduated from the RBH in 1960. She recalled an experience when she was working as a nurse in Brisbane for a company that also employed tradesmen. The men went on strike when they discovered she was not a union member, so she rang Pixie and told her, 'Pay my money, get me in the RANF', which Pixie duly organised. The strike was soon called off. According to Fran, this was typical of the lengths Pixie would go to, to help out a friend.

In 1963, Pixie was appointed a member of the Queensland Nurses' Registration Board, one of two nurse representatives on the five-member board. It was a position she would occupy for 13 years. It brought her into close contact with male-dominated bureaucracy, and sometimes conflict, accustomed as she was to speaking her mind. In Australia at that time, official discrimination against women was still entrenched in the setting of wages, with women continuing to earn substantially less than men in all occupations. Wages for nurses, even in senior positions such as matrons, were poor. Serving on the Nurses' Registration Board and her increasing responsibilities with the RANF gave Pixie a wider insight into the problems of nurse training around the state, and she was determined to do something about it.

For the first time, she also had close contact with the Sisters of Mercy, who had established the Mater public and private hospitals in South Brisbane. The division between Catholics and non-Catholics was still pronounced in Queensland society, and this was reflected in limited interaction between nurses who worked in these two distinct systems: state and Catholic. Pixie, however, was to develop good relationships with nurse managers such as Sister Angela Mary, who became sister administrator of the three Mater hospitals in 1966. She recalled: 'They were great members of the RANF and active on many of our committees.'

During her employment at the RANF, Pixie had advocated for better pay and recognition for the important job of a charge nurse, and had made efforts to have this position separately recognised in the Nurses' Award that was set by the Conciliation and Arbitration Commission, the forerunner of the Queensland Industrial Relations Commission.

'When I left the RANF to join St Andrew's, Bartz Schultz, who had been the senior nurse educator at the RBH, took over from me as secretary. She was a highly decorated army nurse from World War II, and she did an amazing job for the RANF in Queensland. Shortly after she started, she rang me to say she was going to continue that effort to get the charge nurse position recognised in the Nurses' Award. To demonstrate why this was so important, she got permission to take Commissioner Philip Self on a tour of the Brisbane General Hospital, starting in casualty. Here, in the midst of mayhem every day, was the charge nurse, Sister Florence Bourke. She was a married woman with two children, about 5 foot 11, rather plump, and somehow her veil was always a bit skew. But she was always calm and pleasant, an extraordinary woman, in fact. She used to fold her arms and then unfold them as though she was directing traffic, saying, "Doctor, there's a patient over there …", "Would you see that patient …", "Nurse, would you …", and this went on all day. Bourke made sure everybody was looked after. Mr Self was standing there in his expensive suit and he was looking at all of this – people coming in, bleeding and needing sutures, some had been in car accidents, and on and on it went. Bartz left him standing there for a while before she introduced him to Sister Bourke. He asked her, "Is it always like this, Sister?" She folded her arms again and said, "Actually, it's a quiet day today". He turned to Bartz and said, "You've got your classification. I've never seen anything like it. It's the nearest approach to hell I've ever seen!" Bourke never batted an eyelid. Mr Self rather sheepishly invited Bartz to lunch at Lennon's Hotel – he really could not believe what he had witnessed.'

When she finally retired, Sister Bourke's immense contribution to the hospital was publicly acknowledged by General Medical Superintendent Dr Pye, who pointed out that on some days during the 20 years she did this job, she had organised the care of as many as 1,000 patients a day.

Florence Bourke had trained at the Brisbane General Hospital in the 1930s and had served with the Australian Army Nursing Service during World War II. Pixie had great respect for the 600 Queensland nurses who had served in the war: 'These women who had trained between the wars also served in World War II. The nurses who died on the *Centaur* and the 21 who were massacred near Sumatra after the fall of Singapore sacrificed their lives. I felt it was important to remember and recognise their contribution, and also to acknowledge many of those who continued to teach student nurses in the hospitals after the war. We were never told about their contribution.'

The status of army nurses was elevated within the community in 1951 with the formation of the Royal Australian Army Nursing Corps (RAANC), and a year later the Citizens Military Forces company (CMF) was created to train reservists for call up in an emergency. Volunteers were required to attend 12 days of compulsory training each year, and at least one 14-day camp. A long-held objective of army nurse training was to ensure nurses were 'efficient', and for this they needed to attain certain standards of nursing practice and competence in the organisation of military hospitals. This had been the way nurses had been trained in the military since World War I, and 40 years later not much had changed. When Pixie applied and was accepted for the CMF in 1957, training was focused on nursing and also military administration.

She had decided to join the CMF with a friend, Joan Lefrancke, who was working at the Women's Hospital: 'It was her idea. She said to me, "What about it? Perhaps we should do it".'

Deciding to 'do it' became a big commitment and an important part of Pixie's life for the next nine years. In addition to an annual two-week camp, CMF members attended a parade every Thursday night. Members of the Nursing Corps regularly sat for examinations in subjects including military law and administration, and Pixie progressed over the years to the rank of major, equivalent to the position of a hospital matron.

She viewed her service as continuing her family's tradition of military service, and the CMF had a connection for her to the 25th Battalion in which her father and uncles had served. After World War II, the 49th Battalion and 25th Battalion had been re-established as Citizens Military Forces, part of the reorganisation of military service at a time when the world was gripped by the Cold War. The Nursing Corps was one of the few avenues open to women who had an interest in military service. Young men, on the other hand, were required to complete national service in the army, navy or air force, as Australian forces in the 1950s were called up for duty in Malaysia, Korea, Borneo and Vietnam.

CMF camps were held at Greenbank, also the site for camps for school cadets and some training of the regular army. The Greenbank site was a canvas camp, made up of ablution blocks, storage buildings, an open hardstand area, field kitchens and tents. Much of the cooking was done with a Wiles Cooker, and cooks who knew how to use these cookers were highly sought after. Showering arrangements were also rudimentary. The nurses used 'donkey boilers', originally used on ships and so named because they resembled the shape of a donkey. The body of the donkey was a 40-gallon drum that was kept full of water. A fire underneath the drum heated the water. To extract hot water, a lever was turned to let in more cold water, causing the hot water to overflow down a spout and thus providing a supply of hot water for the volunteers.

'Camp was always in August and it was either raining and freezing, or fine with the Westerlies blowing, and dust everywhere. It was basic out there, but we enjoyed it. The cadets would come into the camp and some got quite ill with diseases like mumps or measles, or they would get hurt in accidents and require medical attention. We had quite a busy time in the hospital, which was made of big canvas tents.

'We also had to teach groups of "junior nurses" or people who were in quite good office jobs in "Civvy Street". Most of them were older than me, but they were very receptive and I enjoyed training them. In the Army Nursing Corps I sat exams regularly. I was particularly interested in military law and did quite well in that, and I learnt a lot about army nursing, which appealed to me.'

The Army Nursing Corps members slept in tents, and one night her army colleagues discovered something her other nursing colleagues had long known about Pixie – her tendency to sleepwalk.

'I was sharing a tent with another captain, and I thought someone had called me up to the hospital. I got up in the middle of the night and got dressed, including putting on the veil, and off I went to the hospital. The guards were sitting around braziers for warmth because it was freezing out there. They saluted me and I said I was going up to the hospital. When I got up there the Nursing Sergeant said to me, "What are you doing up here?" And I said, "You called me". She realised I was sleepwalking.

'It's a funny sort of thing, you don't realise you're asleep. I was quite conscious; I had addressed those fellas as I walked up there. So then I had to walk back; you should have seen the look on their faces when they saw me return, because I had only been up at the hospital for a few minutes. I got all my gear off and got back into bed. In the morning I heard my tent mate say, "Who the hell's had my uniform on?" Of course, I'd picked hers up. We liked them to be all nice and ironed. She said to me, "Did you walk in your sleep?" I said , "Yes", and she said, "Next time use your own damn uniform". I think it was the only time I ever did [sleepwalk] at camp.'

Another standard activity during army camps was route-marches. At one of her first camps, the colonel asked Pixie to lead the Nursing Corps on a route-march, with an accompanying army band.

'Nobody told me that you went quite slowly because the band had to keep up. We went up past the school at Greenbank, and we were covering the entire marching route at a good pace when suddenly the band stopped. This young officer came up to me and asked me whether I would mind marching more slowly – they were running out of puff. I thought I was supposed to go on a route-march and be back by a certain time. I thought the faster we did it the better, but the poor old band members were exhausted! I complied and we marched slowly back.'

Every Thursday night, Pixie attended a parade that was held from 6.00 pm to 8.00 pm at Water Street in Fortitude Valley. The CMF parades took place on a historic site – during World War II it had been used as one of the depots for the processing of volunteers who had enlisted, and during the war volunteer defence corps members also received training there. The drill hall was the venue for many social events of a military nature, such as mess dinners.

Pixie recalled that one Friday morning following a parade, a young nurse who had seen her go out in uniform the previous evening said, 'Excuse me, Sister, which war were you in?' Pixie said, 'I could have punched her on the nose, I was all of about 32 in those days!'

Pixie was indeed still a young woman who had demonstrated leadership capability, in both her nursing and part-time army careers. After three years away from the clinical coalface, Pixie was once again ready for a change in direction.

## Chapter 5

# Taking the Reins at St Andrew's

### 1965–1970

A lifetime working and contributing to something you love. That's easy enough to say, but words don't convey the commitment Pixie had to St Andrew's War Memorial Hospital. To be appointed at just 35 years of age as matron was a considerable achievement. Beginning in 1965, Pixie would spend 27 years at St Andrew's, 13 as matron (or director of nursing) and then 14 as CEO, and it was at this hospital that she came into her own as a leader and manager.

Although an Anglican, Pixie appreciated the vision of the Assembly of the Presbyterian Church of Queensland, which envisaged a hospital as a living memorial to Australians who had served and sacrificed in the two world wars. The idea of commemoration resonated with many people. Presbyterian congregations throughout Queensland, as well as the wider public who responded to doorknock and other appeals, gave generously to help raise the £300,000 target set to establish St Andrew's. Contributions great and small helped fill the savings fund, and in 1958, little more than a decade after first being mooted, St Andrew's opened its doors. Three doctors – Dr Cecil Black, Dr Harold Crawford and his colleague Dr Alex Mayes – who were members of the Presbyterian Church in Brisbane played a significant role in helping to establish the hospital. They were part of the church's Hospital Enquiry Committee formed in 1946, and they lent their practical support for many years.

A number of sites were identified for the new hospital, and in the late 1940s the Presbyterian Church purchased a 1.2-hectare site for the hospital at Herston near the medical school, as well as a 4.2-hectare site at Wavell Heights for a future nursing home. Both properties were later sold, and in 1956 land and buildings were bought from another Presbyterian-related institution, Emmanuel College in Spring Hill, as the site of the new hospital. The Scottish heritage so dear to the Presbyterians was permanently made a part of St Andrew's with the adoption of the national flag of Scotland as its emblem when the hospital was opened.

The new 84-bed hospital with medical, surgical and paediatric wards on Wickham Terrace was built alongside the distinctive two-storey building that had housed Emmanuel College before it relocated to the University of Queensland's St Lucia campus in 1955. St Andrew's also opened a 20-bed psychiatric section, known as Terrace Hospital, in a separate house next to the college building, and a maternity ward was added to the main hospital shortly after St Andrew's opened. Over the years of change and expansion, buildings would come and go, but the solid Emmanuel College building remained. It was in this building that Pixie's office and flat, and other nurse accommodation, was located.

The official opening and dedication of the hospital on 17 May 1958 by the Governor of Queensland, Sir Henry Abel Smith, was an important occasion in Brisbane. The opening was attended by more than 3,000 people and was a huge credit to the first chairman of the Board of Governors, Dr Crawford, who died just four months later. His good friend Dr Mayes succeeded him and became the long-time chairman, and he was one of the people instrumental in attracting Pixie to the hospital.

Dr Mayes was a much-admired general practitioner in Brisbane who had served in World War II as a regimental medical officer with the 25th Battalion in the Middle East. He had a flare for project management – in addition to his involvement with the building program at St Andrew's, he chaired the Australian Medical Association Building Committee during its major building program in Herston. By the early 1960s, he had outgrown his busy GP rooms in Clayfield and had relocated his practice to Centaur House, where Pixie also worked as secretary of the RANF. In early 1965, he strolled into Pixie's office to inform her that the first matron of St Andrew's, Miss Dorothea Harrison, was leaving.

'Miss Harrison was a capable ex-Australian Army Nursing Service sister, and I had first met her when she was the student nurse representative on the RANF State Council, when students were not able to sit on the governing body. During her five years at St Andrew's, the number of beds had increased to

148, there were four operating theatres and the nursing school had started. She had also managed the opening of an intensive care section, and was just a terrific person. Dr Mayes asked me to put in an application as matron and I told him, "I don't know if I could do that at the moment. I'll think about it". He said, "Well, Dr Jamieson would like you to", and so I did.'

It was for a good reason that Pixie could not say no: her respect for Dr Ken Jamieson. His achievements in neurosurgery had long marked him as an exceptional man. He was appointed to the Royal Brisbane Hospital (RBH) in 1956, establishing the Department of Neurology and Neurosurgery there in the early 1960s. Dr Jamieson possessed prodigious energy, and his team-focused approach to managing patients was ahead of its time. He encouraged involving nurses, radiologists, neurologists and anaesthetists in the treatment of neurosurgical patients, and also supported improved training for nurses. Pixie had encountered Dr Jamieson when she was charge sister of the private wards at the RBH. Like everyone who knew Dr Jamieson, she respected his intellect, his considerable research achievements, his capacity as a doctor and especially his commitment to patients.

'Dr Jamieson worked harder than any doctor I have ever known. He commanded the greatest respect, and knowing that both Dr Jamieson and Dr Mayes thought I was up to the job of matron persuaded me to put in my application.'

In addition to his role at the RBH, Dr Jamieson shared an operating list one day each week at St Andrew's. He was also a devout Presbyterian, a member of the Board of Governors of St Andrew's and chair of the hospital's Planning Committee. In these positions, he worked closely with Pixie and she appreciated the support he gave her.

Pixie recounted that her entry to St Andrew's in 1965 was 'far from grand'. The day Dr Mayes informed her that she was the successful applicant, she broke her left ankle running up the stairs at the back of the family home in Windsor, and this delayed her appointment by two months.

Shortly before she began her new job in August 1965, Dr Mayes took her on a tour of the hospital. She was astonished when he greeted each staff member, from doctors to nurses, kitchen staff to laundry workers, by name. There was a personal approach at St Andrew's.

Ceremony always had a special place at St Andrew's, particularly in the early decades. And so Pixie's appointment included an official welcome, attended by the Board of Governors, the moderator, the Reverend Crowe and Mrs Crowe, the Appeal Committee, the Women's Auxiliary, the Sewing Circle and the Jumble Sales Committee. All these people played a big part in the success of St Andrew's.

'The first thing I found out about the hospital was what marvellous staff they had, and so I set out to try to ensure these staff never left.

'Miss Harrison had been a very precise lady and I was only 35 when I was appointed. So it was a bit of a shock to the system, I think. And into the bargain I wasn't a Presbyterian.

'However, I had worked with a lot of the doctors at the RBH, so I knew what their requirements and standards were. One of the first things I felt was necessary was to appoint a registered nurse as the bookings sister. So if a doctor rang about a patient with a specific condition who needed admission, the booking sister would know immediately what was required for admission.'

Pixie knew exactly whom she wanted for this job – Sister Ivy Trede, a respected 'block' sister at the RBH, credited with 'teaching' many of the young doctors about patient care in the wards there.

'I bumped into her just after I went to St Andrew's and I said, "How's life?" She said, "Pixie, I just can't walk around that hospital anymore, my knees are so painful". They kept putting her on night duty because she was so efficient. She played a big role in running the whole hospital. So I said that if she was thinking of leaving, I'd like her to consider the job as the bookings sister at St Andrew's. And it was the best day's work I ever did. She had the complete confidence of the doctors, she was absolutely terrific. She was there for about 15 years, and in the last few years she became assistant director of nursing at St Andrew's.'

Pixie was pleased at the prospect of being back among the patients, and had little understanding of the financial pressures facing St Andrew's and many other private hospitals. One of the early casualties of the new hospital was the Maternity Wing. In 1966, 777 babies were born, but it was a financial disaster, and so in May of that year, the 28-bed wing was closed.

'Dr Mayes said to me early on, "You know we've got an overdraft?" I had never been involved with an overdraft, and I said, "Why have we got an overdraft?" I thought I was simply the director of nursing, but I soon found out that in this position you were seen as the face of the hospital. And that's how I got involved with the appeals and fundraising.'

Getting 'involved with the fundraising' gives just a hint of Pixie's skill in raising money. She became a highly successful fundraiser, with a great feel for how to communicate and appeal to people from all walks of life. She worked very closely with the appeals director, Stan Slater.

Success in fundraising, according to Pixie, required good teamwork, and she believed St Andrew's War Memorial Hospital's capacity to survive financial stress at certain times was also thanks to an excellent board, chaired for 25 years by Dr Mayes. 'We had a very good board. They made sure the resources were there to look after patients and that we had sufficient staff. That made a huge difference. The board consisted of a broad group of people who actually listened to each other, people like Mrs GA McLean, who had owned her own private hospital, and Dr Mayes as chairman was superb.'

Many people contributed to the fundraising efforts, which were not confined to Brisbane. From the outset of the planning of St Andrew's, supporters travelled across Queensland, visiting Presbyterian churches, and gathering support from businesses and publicity from newspapers in the quest for funds. House-to-house collections, or doorknock appeals, were adopted early on as a method of raising money, and these collections continued for many years. In 1965, shortly before Pixie joined St Andrew's, the doorknock appeal, known as Field Day, raised £12,000, promising that the hospital would expand and was 'open to all and free to the needy'. The annual and later biannual Scottish Fairs, held in the Brisbane City Hall basement, reflected the hospital's Scottish flavour and traditions. A leading dignitary, such as a Queensland MP or the premier's wife, usually opened the fair, and the official party were piped in before the serving of a particular delicacy of the fair – the haggis – which was made every year by Dr Mayes. The St Andrew's Women's Auxiliary was central to these events, and it was these dedicated women who organised the various stalls: they collected jumble for the jumble sales stall; and their needlework, pickles, jams and chutneys and other goods were the mainstay of the products sold at the fair.

'From the outset the St Andrew's Women's Auxiliary, which later became the St Andrew's Auxiliary, played a vital role in supporting the hospital. It is amazing to think that these women sewed a lot of the items that the hospital used when it opened, including curtains, theatre wear and bed linen.'

A sewing room had been set up on the lower floor of the old cottage the hospital owned, on the corner of North Street. RBH Matron Adelaide Billing, who had trained with Pixie's mother, gave the sewing group patterns for theatre gowns and other garments used in operating theatres. There were two sewing groups, known as the Wednesday and the Thursday ladies, and they also sewed all the curtains for the new wards for the hospital. Later, when construction of the new eye unit began, the sewing group moved to another cottage on the corner of Bradley Street, and they continued to work and sew for St Andrew's for many years.

The Scottish Fairs, doorknock appeals and jumble sales would, in the decades to come, give way to different kinds of fundraising efforts, but whatever the method employed, success always depended on good connections with people. And particularly in the early years, the work of the Auxiliary and other supporters not only assisted the hospital in practical ways, it also helped weave the community into the fabric of St Andrew's.

'Bequests were another important source of funds. The Simpson family, for example, made an important bequest to establish the eye unit in 1974. The family were very generous, and a Scottish family. The fact that St Andrew's was part of the Scottish society, as it were, often brought us significant donations, particularly in the 1960s and 1970s.'

St Andrew's also had supporters in high places, and this included the Premier of Queensland, Frank Nicklin, who visited St Andrew's early in 1967, where he was taken on a tour of the hospital conducted by Pixie and Dr Mayes; and the premier, of course, knew the Annat family very well from their Palmwoods days. The untimely death of his wife Georgina (Ina) at the Mater Private Hospital in 1966 spurred the hospital into establishing a room in her memory as a place for patients' families when they had to wait at the hospital at critical times: 'The Ina Nicklin Room was always full of patients' relatives who were waiting to see loved ones. They could have a cup of tea and a sandwich, it was somewhere comfortable for them to wait.'

Pixie's job as director of nursing not only introduced her to hospital finances and clinical care, it also involved her directly in one of her continuing interests: nurse education. The hospital's School for Nursing Training made St Andrew's one of the first private hospitals in Queensland to be registered for nurse training when it opened in September 1958. The tutor sister, Joan Coyer, an accomplished ex-Toowoomba Hospital nurse who was supported in teaching students by St Andrew's charge sisters and registered nurses, ran the School for Nursing Training. While not as rigid as the RBH, nurse training at St Andrew's nevertheless emphasised old-fashioned 'discipline'. 'Smartly uniformed and crisp' was, in Pixie's view, a good barometer of a training hospital, and she recounted that Dr Jamieson once commented how students came to the hospital as 'kids' and graduated as highly accomplished young women. The presence of 135 or so students at St Andrew's at any one time encouraged a culture of learning, and visiting doctors provided lectures to the students.

'We were fortunate that many of the experienced specialists who consulted at St Andrew's freely gave up their time to educate our students. We also introduced clinical instructors, the first of whom was a former student nurse at the St Andrew's Nursing School. In that way, registered nurses in the wards had help instructing students.'

In the early years at St Andrew's, some of the tasks student nurses were required to do harked back to rather tedious domestic chores that nurses had reluctantly performed for decades, such as folding towels so that all the folds lined up exactly, cutting up butters and setting up jam for trays, carbolising beds following the discharge of a patient, and boiling pan covers, catheters and face masks: 'The hospital laundry went out to Bishops, a professional launderer, but the student nurses had to sponge out any soiling of the sheets and drawsheets beforehand. The sheets had to be stain-free before going to Bishops.'

The young trainees also had a great deal of contact with patients soon after commencing their training, and they progressed rapidly to becoming competent nurses – graduate nurses from St Andrew's had a reputation for being well trained. There were many student nurses who remained at the hospital for many years after graduating, including two sisters, Libby and Hilary Harlin Brown, and a mother and daughter who qualified at St Andrew's, Marion and Robyn Bourne. Pixie, of course, has a host of stories from her many years of interacting with student nurses.

'There was one young woman who was extremely sweet, but we always felt she was not quite cut out to be a nurse. She came on night duty almost late one night. She had her uniform on but was wearing a pair of gold spike-heeled shoes. The noise was unbelievable in the quiet of the night. She eventually borrowed a pair of slippers from a patient and the next morning she put the gold shoes back on and off she went. Her aunt was an interior designer and she later became an assistant in the business.'

Pixie recalled interviewing scores of student nurse applicants, including a young woman from far western Queensland who, when asked why she wanted to become a nurse, replied, 'I love looking after sick animals'. According to Pixie, she was one of the best nurses St Andrew's ever trained.

As Pixie often recounted, there were occasions when roles were changed; when people of very high station became patients themselves and thus had the opportunity to see the workings of medical care from another point of view.

On one such occasion, the highly regarded Dr Jamieson himself came to St Andrew's for a procedure.

'He was due to come in at about three o'clock in the afternoon. My phone went at about 3.30 pm. The sister in charge of the ward said, "You had better come down, you've got one very upset neurosurgeon down here". I said, "Oh, my goodness, what's happened?" The sister said she had instructed a student nurse to make sure the wards and beds were ready for some new patients that afternoon, and pointed out that one of them was Dr Ken Jamieson. To mention Dr Jamieson to the student nurses was like mentioning a god. This young nurse had stewed on this all day, apparently. She decided to avoid meeting the star patient by any means. She rushed into what she thought was the next room, where there was a gentleman sitting in an easy chair. She asked him, "Do you mind if I hide in your cupboard?" He was startled and said, "Yes, Nurse, but why would you want to?" She said to him, "There is this doctor, Dr Jamieson, coming in and I'm terrified of him". He said, "Sit down, Nurse, I am Dr Jamieson". She let out a scream that the sister heard at the other end of the ward. When I walked into his room, Ken Jamieson was sitting in the chair like a stunned mullet. He said he had no idea that the girls were frightened of him. I said, "Ken, they're not so much frightened of you, they just hold you in such respect". I said to the sister, "Give him a nice stiff Scotch and he'll be right". And so he was, but he couldn't get over it and he often mentioned this incident to me. The student nurse eventually became a highly respected artist in Western Australia.'

Pixie's prescription of a stiff drink in such circumstances showed she appreciated the practical value of an occasional Scotch, but she recalled that the Presbyterians did not always see it the same way:

'One of the Presbyterian ministers came up to see me in my flat in St Andrew's. He saw this Johnny Walker bottle sitting in the cabinet and he said, "Pixie, what are you doing with that?" I said, "Oh, I sit here and I have my Scotch and I watch the news at 10.30 at night". I told Dr Mayes, and he joked, "Don't take the slightest notice of them. Some of them have so much grog in their own houses they couldn't jump over it". I said, "I'm aware that I'm on church property". They had never said anything to me before about this. And we couldn't have raffles either.'

At St Andrew's, Pixie once again took a keen interest in the Student Nurses Unit that she had helped to establish as a young student nurse. In Queensland, there were active Student Nurses Units in many hospitals. At the RBH, by far still the largest single employer of nurses, student nurses were concerned about inadequate training as well as duties which they felt had nothing to do with nursing. A student nurse conference held in 1968, attended also by student nurses from St Andrew's, helped propel the RANF to take more concerted action towards tackling long-standing problems in nursing education as well as employment and living conditions. At a hospital level, Pixie found herself in a similar position to other matrons: they had hospitals to run, patients to care for and doctors to keep happy. As a leader in the RANF, Pixie was committed to improving nurse education and working conditions, but she had to also fulfil her role as a senior manager at St Andrew's. She did her best to balance these competing interests.

'It wasn't always easy, but I think the kids appreciated that someone was interested in these issues. I couldn't do anything that would prejudice the hospital with the Health Department. And that was a balancing act. It didn't stop me doing things, but I had to be aware of this.'

After Pixie left her full-time job at the RANF to join St Andrew's, she continued to serve on the RANF Executive Committee in Queensland for 14 years, serving as RANF Queensland President from 1967 until 1969. The big focus during these years was to lift the standard of nurse training, which brought Pixie into direct conflict with 'the bureaucrats', including the Health Minister and his department.

'The bureaucrats didn't have a clue. In a lot of the discussions, it always came down to money. The student nurses were the main workforce and, of course, they lived in the nurses' quarters. From the discussion, you would have thought nurses lived in Buckingham Palace the way they went on.'

One of the chief protagonists in these years of argument was the Director-General of the Health Department, Dr Abraham Fryberg, the man who once told Pixie that nurses were expected to rub backs and carry bedpans. Dr Fryberg, while respected particularly by doctors, often took decisions that made him unpopular. He was once publicly called 'a little dictator', and commented that he only objected to this label because it included the word 'little'. It was then no surprise that he would bump heads with another person small in stature and large in intellect, Pixie, who from a young age had shown herself quite capable of speaking her mind.

'Dr Fryberg was a difficult man to deal with from a nursing and private hospital viewpoint. We had many pointed discussions while he was the director-general.'

Another episode where her feisty approach was evident involved her clash with the chairman of the Queensland Nurses' Registration Board, Dr P Patrick, and the Minister for Health, Seymour Douglas (Doug) Tooth, over changes to the nursing curriculum proposed in 1968. Just as during the early 1960s, when curriculum changes were introduced without proper consultation with nurse representatives, once again in 1968 the Registration Board formed a curriculum subcommittee without informing Pixie, who was one of the two nurse representatives on the board. She was furious when Minister Tooth told the Queensland Parliament that a subcommittee to redraft the curriculum of general training had been formed, with Pixie's support. In a letter to the minister, Pixie pointed out that she had been deliberately excluded by the Registration Board and had no knowledge that a new subcommittee was about to redraft the curriculum. There were exchanges between the minister and Dr Patrick on the one hand, and Pixie and Mrs Violet Hall, president of the RANF Queensland, on the other. In October 1968, Pixie resigned as a member of the Regulations Committee. The issue continued to attract press coverage, with the minister going so far in the Queensland Parliament as to accuse some unnamed RANF officers of having a hidden agenda aimed at scuppering improvements to nurse training. He also claimed there was a hidden 'rather shadowy group of seniors' guiding the 'unrepresentative' Student Nurses Unit into making alarming statements about harm being done to patients.

It was somewhat surprising that Pixie, who hardly regarded herself as a firebrand, and who came from conservative country roots, was in the camp of the RANF 'troublemakers'. The row was eventually smoothed over, and Pixie continued to provide input into the curriculum review. In 1969, the period of nurse training was reduced from four to three years, and it was agreed that lectures would be held during working hours. In 1970, the number of lecture hours for nurse trainees were substantially increased.

While bedding down improvements at St Andrew's and continuing her campaigning for nurses through the RANF, Pixie also felt she would benefit from further study. In 1968, with the support of the board, she took a year's leave from St Andrew's to study a diploma course in Nursing Administration at the College of Nursing Australia (Queensland), which had its campus in the grounds of the Princess Alexandra Hospital. Pixie absorbed this additional management training with ease, and she felt it increased her abilities as a nursing and hospital manager. In the few years since commencing at St Andrew's, Pixie had become an experienced manager and lobbyist for nurses. These skills would stand her in good stead for the challenging decades ahead.

# Chapter 6

# Breaking New Ground

## 1971–1979

By 1970, St Andrew's was a well-established private hospital and a familiar landmark on Wickham Terrace, which was the dividing boundary between Spring Hill and the city. This elevated, S-shaped street often confused first-time visitors coming to the hospital because it looped around two blocks – the higher street where St Andrew's was located and lower Wickham Terrace, which had become a medical hub for many specialists. Wickham Terrace was also home to Pixie's first-floor flat in the administration building (formerly the Emmanuel College building), where some other senior nurses also lived.

'Spring Hill was a quiet, convenient suburb, although I also went home every weekend to our family home – we sold our Windsor house in 1978 and I bought a smaller house in Everton Hills. It was useful to live on-site during the week at St Andrew's because I was always available if there was an emergency or problem – there was only one bomb scare in all the time I worked at St Andrew's.'

Every ward and operating theatre at St Andrew's was kept busy, even during financially challenging times, thanks to the patronage of hundreds of visiting specialists who performed surgery or referred their patients for admission to the hospital. Every ward contained countless stories, far too many to tell. One ward that was close to Pixie's heart was the children's ward, on the first floor of the Northern Wing; it was small but in high demand, largely due to able management by Sister Margaret 'Peg' Sullivan.

Margaret Sullivan, like Pixie, had trained at the Royal Brisbane Hospital (RBH) and graduated in 1958. She won a highly prized Nestlé travelling scholarship, and her overseas studies increased her interest and experience in paediatric nurse management. She joined St Andrew's in 1960, and painstakingly planned the paediatric ward that opened in 1964.

Her early death in October 1970 in St Andrew's was felt deeply by Pixie and her other medical and nursing colleagues.

'Margaret Sullivan was an outstanding paediatric nurse. But more than this, she truly cared for those children in her ward. There were daily scenes in the paediatric ward that just wouldn't happen these days. She would be writing a report with children in her lap and other kids would be standing on chairs, peering over her shoulders to see what she was doing. She was a pioneer in paediatric nursing care in Queensland. Peg could be very persuasive, and as a result she convinced Dr Swiss Davies to operate on a little boy from Lismore called Stephen who had a severe cleft palate and harelip and walked with the aid of a walker donated privately by one of the doctors. As part of his surgical care, Dr Davies ordered a special prosthesis for his palate from the Children's Dental Hospital. Two days after the surgery, Peg was feeding Stephen strained porridge for breakfast. Dr Davies walked into the ward and said, "Good morning, Sister, how is Stephen?" Stephen gave a shriek of delight when he saw Dr Davies, and out fell the palate. Unperturbed, Peg replied, "Good morning, Doctor, the palate is in the porridge". It was a very funny moment. All in all, Stephen was at St Andrew's for about a year, and of course St Andrew's did not charge for his treatment and stay because his family could not afford it.'

Pixie recalled that on 3 October 1970, on the morning her friend Peg died of cancer, she visited her in the hospital and promised Peg that St Andrew's would establish a special fund in her name. True to Pixie's word, the Margaret Sullivan Paediatric Nursing Fund was set up to provide scholarships to Queensland paediatric nurses and dedicated to improving children's patient care. Pixie was also instrumental in setting up an inter-hospital paediatric nursing committee, which later became the Paediatric Nursing Association in Queensland, bringing together paediatric nurses from the state, Catholic and private hospitals. Margaret Sullivan's contribution to St Andrew's was also recognised when the children's ward was named the Margaret Sullivan Paediatric Unit in 1977 at a dedication ceremony attended by her parents. This legacy of remembrance continued for many decades, and later the Australian Confederation of Paediatric and Child Health Nurses took over the management of the Margaret Sullivan scholarship.

Many doctors who consulted at the RBH, including the Royal Children's Hospital in Herston, also saw patients at St Andrew's. Pixie's medical connections included obstetrician Dr Harold Horn and his daughter, paediatrician Dr Marie Jameson. Marie said she was always impressed by Pixie at St Andrew's: 'She buzzed around making sure everything was working properly. Nothing was ever too much trouble for her.'

Other friends, some of them ex-nurses from the RBH, recalled Pixie's kindness when they encountered her at St Andrew's. Claudia Sharpe came to know Pixie well when they trained together at the RBH, and many years later she booked into St Andrew's for surgery performed by Dr Brian Courtice. Hospital stays of ten days or more were still the norm for many procedures, and Claudia's doctor insisted she remain in the hospital for 12 days. It was the Christmas season and, with a young family of her own by then, Claudia was not thrilled at the prospect of spending Christmas in hospital. She was cheered up by frequent visits from the St Andrew's choir singing Christmas carols. There was 'a family atmosphere', and Claudia suspected Pixie had instigated much of the cheer. She had an ability to be careful with detail, yet seldom overlooked personal situations.

Anyone who worked, volunteered or consulted at St Andrew's from its earliest days was familiar with the myriad alterations and additions made to the hospital. Over the years, the St Andrew's board managed the purchase of surrounding land so that the hospital would eventually occupy the entire block – bound by Wickham Terrace on its high southern side, Boundary Street at the foot of the hill and two narrow side roads, North and Bradley streets. The only certainty about the environment at St Andrew's was constant change and improvement, driven by an enthusiastic board and the Planning Committee chaired by Dr Jamieson. After the hospital's opening in 1958, the next big change was the Northern Wing, completed in 1964, which added more medical and surgical beds and housed the hospital's new intensive care unit. By 1974, the North Street Wing was completed to accommodate, among other things, a new surgical ward and the eye unit.

Pixie recalled phoning Dr Pye, still general medical superintendent of the RBH, to discuss the acquisition of a microscope for ophthalmic surgery: 'This was fairly early on in my time at St Andrew's, and he said to me, "It will cost you thousands", which was an awful lot of money in those days. He said, "You'll never make any money out of it". I said, "I'm not here to make money out of it, we're here to give a service".'

The Royal Brisbane Hospital complex, 1940s.

Lady Lamington Nurses' Home, Royal Brisbane Hospital, in the 1950s.

FOLLOWING PAGES: Christmas celebrations in Ward 4E, Royal Brisbane Hospital, 1958. Pixie is in the front row (left).

Pixie with Jim Cobhan, at the Royal Ball for Princess Alexandra of Kent, Brisbane City Hall, 1959 (above) and in 1960 (right).

Pixie with a male officer at a Citizen Military Forces (CMF) camp at Greenbank, Brisbane, in 1959.

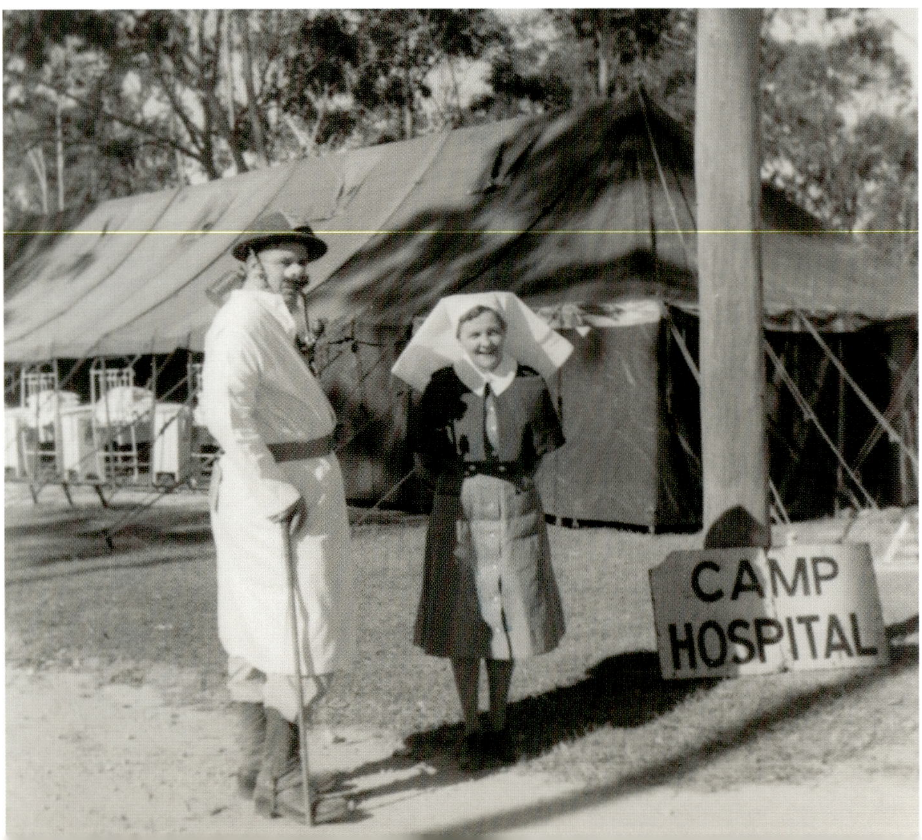

## BRISBANE'S SCOTTISH FAIR

Lady May Abel Smith, official guest at Brisbane's Scottish Fair, tours the stalls. Accompanied by the President of the St. Andrew's War Memorial Hospital Women's Auxiliary, Mrs. A. J. Collins, Lady May showed great interest in every aspect of the Fair. Here Lady May purchases glorious crucifix orchids from Mrs. N. Lacey.

St Andrew's Scottish Fairs (featured in the *St Andrew's Messenger*) were held regularly to raise funds for the hospital. The Queensland Governor's wife, Lady May Abel Smith, was the official guest at the 1960 fair.

Ellen (Ellie) married Bruce Murr in Port Moresby in 1961.

Ward 4E's 1962 Christmas party. Pixie is third from the right and her second-in-charge and very good friend Fran Ryan is second from the right.

Pixie's father, Jim Annat, with his grandson, Peter Murr, at the family home in Windsor, 1964.

Happy moment of the signing of the contract for the £200,000 extensions to St. Andrew's. From left: the Rev. R. H. C. Crowe (Clerk of the Assembly), Mr. V. S. Wyllie (the chairman of the Appeals Committee), Mr. R. S. Byrnes (the General Secretary and Assembly Treasurer) and Dr. Alex Mayes (the Chairman of the Board of Governors).

The signing of a contract for extensions to St Andrew's was reported in the *St Andrew's Messenger* in 1963. Left to right: Rev. Crowe, Victor Wylie, RS Byrnes and board chairman Dr Alex Mayes.

St Andrew's War Memorial Hospital on Wickham Terrace, Spring Hill, 1960s.

# News at St. Andrew's

## Secretary of R.A.N.F. Accepts Post . . .

**The new Matron of St. Andrew's War Memorial Hospital, Miss Isobel Annat, returns to the demands of Hospital work after three years on the staff of the Royal Australian Nursing Federation (Queensland Branch) of which she was appointed Executive Secretary last year.**

Miss Annat takes over from Acting Matron, Sister Phyllis Hughes in July.

Expert knowledge of Queensland nursing conditions has been combined with overseas experience in Miss Annat's career.

Miss Annat received her own training at the Brisbane General Hospital from 1948 to 1952, and then made an overseas working tour of two-and-a-half years.

On returning she went back to the Brisbane General Hospital, and was in charge of the Intermediate Ward for five years before going to the R.A.N.F.

Miss Annat is in the C.M.F., and holds the rank of Major in the Royal Australian Army Nursing Corps.

"I'm looking forward to St. Andrew's very much, and to being back in the Hospital situation among patients," Miss Annat said.

"And I'm very pleased that St. Andrew's is a training Hospital. The stability of trained staff is particularly important, but I am also very interested in the training of student nurses and their impact on the future of their profession."

But she felt regret at leaving the Nursing Federation, even to do something she expected to be as interesting as her duties at St. Andrew's, Miss Annat said.

The future of nursing, and of every institution for nursing in this State is very much bound up with the prosperity of the R.A.N.F., Miss Annat said.

For the last two years with the R.A.N.F. Miss Annat has been a member of the Nurse's Registration Board, in constant touch with regional training and with the nursing situation throughout the State.

She has also taken part in the activities by the R.A.N.F. and the College of Nursing, Australia (Queensland State Committee) to implement refresher courses for trained nurses.

MISS ISOBEL ANNAT

In June 1965, the *St Andrew's Messenger* announced Pixie's appointment as matron of St Andrew's War Memorial Hospital.

Pixie with her parents, Jim and Madoline, in 1965 at her official welcome to St Andrew's.

Madoline Annat (left) at the Royal Children's Hospital's centenary celebrations in 1967 alongside lifelong nursing friends with whom she trained.

The well-loved cook at St Andrew's, Miss Annie Rushton, in a 1962 article in the *St Andrew's Messenger* reporting her impending trip home to England.

**MISS ANNIE RUSHTON**, who has been cook at St. Andrew's since the opening of the Hospital, with the handbag presented to her before her trip to England.

# THE PREMIER CALLS

**The Premier of Queensland, the Hon. G. F. R. Nicklin, M.M., M.L.A., visited St. Andrew's War Memorial Hospital on January 18.**

Mr. Nicklin was welcomed by the Chairman of the Board of Governors, Dr. Alex Mayes, and the Matron Miss Isobel Annat, and made a two-hour tour of the Hospital with them.

The new surgical suite (see below) was then nearing completion.

The Premier met and chatted with patients in most sections of the Hospital.

One of the very attractive rooms at St. Andrew's is the Mrs. Ina Nicklin Memorial Room, established by Mrs. Nicklin's Welfare Committee in honour of their founder, who was the Premier's wife.

Mr. Nicklin was told of the real service this room performs for relatives of patients who must wait at the Hospital at critical times. Here is one place they are quietly apart from the running of the Hospital, able to rest and talk—and even make themselves a cup of tea.

Later the Premier joined the Board of Governors and hospital staff, with representatives of the Appeals Committee and the Women's Auxiliary for afternoon tea in the Boardroom.

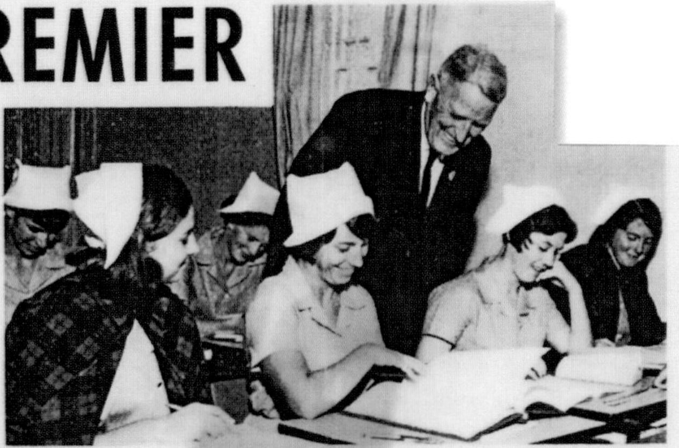

**The Premier visits the nurses' classroom at St. Andrew's. Studying were (left to right, front row) : Nurse N. Roberts, of Mt. Gravatt, Nurse Robyn Stone, of Wilston; Nurse Glenda Lincoln, of Ashgrove, and Nurse Andrea Eklund, of Chelmer. In the second row were : Nurse Susan Allan, of East Brisbane (left), and Nurse Cheryl Mott, of Rochedale.**

ST. ANDREW'S *Messenger*
OFFICIAL JOURNAL OF ST. ANDREW'S WAR MEMORIAL HOSPITAL
G.P.O. Box 764K, Brisbane. VOL. 21. JUNE, 1967.

Premier Frank Nicklin, a great supporter of St Andrew's, visited the hospital in January 1967.

# Specialising — In People

**Awareness of the need for constant review of the care given to patients, and the absolute necessity of being professionally well-informed are two of the factors considered in the Diploma Course in Nursing Administration now being studied by the Matron of St. Andrew's War Memorial Hospital, Miss Isobel Annat.**

**Miss Annat is at present on leave from the Hospital, studying at the College of Nursing, Australia (Queensland Branch), as holder of the Royal Australian Nursing Federation's Scholarship for 1968.**

Psychology, sociology, social structure, and public speaking are included in the course, together with nursing administration, hospital administration, institutional catering, business principles, and nursing history and trends.

Miss Annat said recently that the course will be invaluable when she returns to duty at St. Andrew's. "The student gains a broader picture of the role of the administrator in both nursing service and nursing education," Miss Annat said.

The study of "patients as people" was an important part of the course, and reflected a trend in nursing education to overcome the loss of ordinary personal interactions which could be caused by increasing specialisation in medical treatment.

It is necessary for Hospital and Nursing administrators to be aware of the tremendous amount of knowledge required by the nurse today.

Nurses must have a sound knowledge of people as social beings and always remember that they are helping to treat not only a disease or condition, but the person with that disease or condition.

"An efficient Hospital today is in touch with the world, not cut off from it. The patients don't feel they're in never-never-land," Miss Annat said.

"This necessitates an extension of nursing education to cope with advances in medical science and to ensure that the patient derives benefit from intelligent nursing care."

The following year, the *St Andrew's Messenger* reported that Pixie was taking a year's study leave to attend the College of Nursing Australia in 1968.

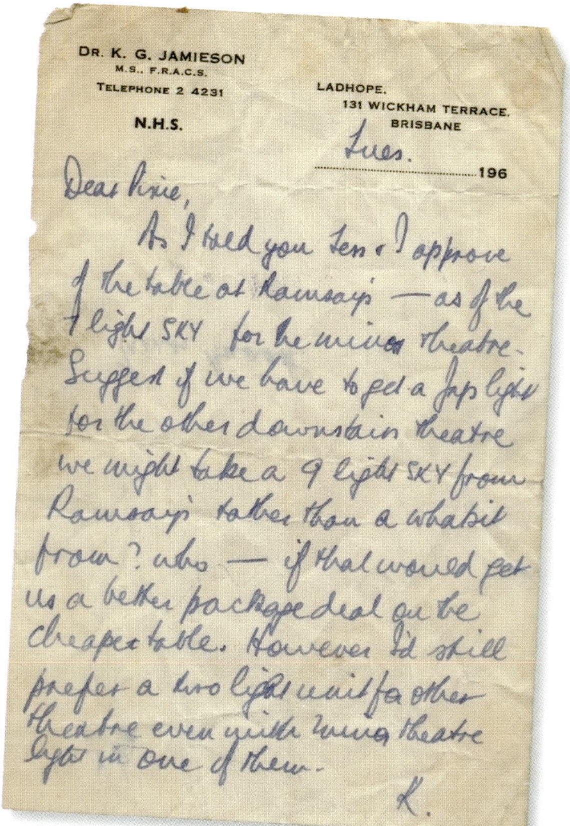

DR. K. G. JAMIESON
M.S., F.R.A.C.S.
TELEPHONE 2 4231
N.H.S.

LADHOPE.
131 WICKHAM TERRACE.
BRISBANE

Tues. ..........196

Dear Pixie,

As I told you Len & I approve of the table at Ramsay's — as of the 4 light SKY for the minor theatre. Suggest if we have to get a Jap light for the other downstairs theatre we might take a 9 light SKY from Ramsay's rather than a whatsit from ? who — if that would get us a better package deal on the cheaper table. However I'd still prefer a two light unit for other theatre even with minor theatre light in one of them.

K.

**ABOVE:** Dr Ken Jamieson.

**RIGHT:** This note from the 1960s written by renowned neurosurgeon Dr Ken Jamieson, chair of the St Andrew's Planning Committee, to Pixie is one of many she received regarding structural changes to the hospital.

**BELOW:** On 27 July 1970, St Andrew's War Memorial Hospital celebrated its 10th year of nursing graduates at St Andrew's Presbyterian Church in Creek Street, Brisbane. Pixie is in the centre with principal nurse educator Joan Coyer to her right.

# MEMORIAL TO SISTER MARGARET SULLIVAN

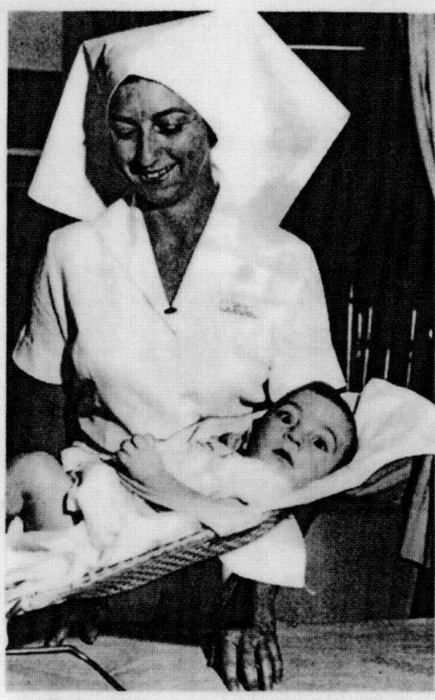

*A skilled specialist at work. the late Sister Margaret Sullivan with a young patient in the Children's Ward at St. Andrew's War Memorial Hospital. Sister Sullivan believed children have a real need to be amused and interested, even during a visit to Hospital, and that this need became important from the age of about 18 months onwards.*

## Career

**Miss Margaret Sullivan's home was Peachester on the North Coast. She graduated as a General Nurse from the Royal Brisbane Hospital in 1957 and studied midwifery at Nambour.**

**She obtained Midwifery and Child Care Certificates while studying at the Brisbane Centre, and was a member of the staff of the Melbourne Children's Hospital for some months before coming to St. Andrew's in 1961.**

Miss Sullivan held a Diploma in Hospital Nursing and Ward Management from the College of Nursing, Australia.

In 1967 she won the Nestle Paediatric Nursing Scholarship for Queensland, which gave her the opportunity for an extended study tour overseas.

At that time Miss Sullivan told "The Messenger" that two subjects of special interest during her tour would be neo-natal care, especially the care of newborn babies with congenital abnormalities, and play therapy for children in hospital.

She intended to get information about specially interesting studies of play therapy which have been carried out in London.

In her opinion, children of all age groups need to be amused and interested, and this need is very important from the age of 18 months.

LEFT: The early death in 1970 of Sister Margaret (Peg) Sullivan was felt deeply by everyone at St Andrew's. To honour this outstanding paediatric nurse, Pixie and her colleagues established the Margaret Sullivan Paediatric Nursing Fund.

BELOW: In March 1973, the Governor of Queensland, Air Marshall Sir Colin Hannah, paid an official visit to St Andrew's. He was considered a very good friend of the hospital.

# THE GOVERNOR CALLS

*His Excellency, The Governor of Queensland, Sir Colin Hannah (right) and Lady Hannah (centre) arrives for an official visit to St. Andrew's War Memorial Hospital. Seen crossing to the entrance steps were (left to right) Hospital Manager, Mr. Ian Morris, the Govenor's Aide, Captain Graham Roberts-Thomson, St. Andrew's Matron, Miss Isobel Annat, Lady Hannah, Lady-in-Waiting, Mrs. M. Bain, the Chairman of the Board, Dr. Alex Mayes, C.B.E., and His Excellency. The Governor and Lady Hannah toured the Hospital.*

RIGHT: The 1972 ceremony to honour the student nurses who graduated from St Andrew's that year.

BELOW: The 1973 student nurse graduation ceremony. Left to right: Joan Coyer, Minister for Health Doug Tooth, graduating nurse Pam Winship, Pixie and Dr Alex Mayes.

**ABOVE:** Pixie worked closely with St Andrew's nurse educator Suzanne Stirling (second from the right).

**LEFT:** As vice-president and later president of the Royal Australian Nursing Federation (RANF), Pixie travelled overseas to attend many professional gatherings, including the 1974 American Nurses Association annual conference in California.

Left to right: Dr Alex Mayes, Mrs Sallyanne Atkinson, Dr Leigh Atkinson, Ron Glenney, Pixie Annat and Stan Slater at a St Andrew's annual dinner in the mid-1970s.

ABOVE: Pixie took her parents on a holiday to New Zealand in 1976.

LEFT: Piper Archie Galloway at the 15th student nurse graduation ceremony held at St Paul's Presbyterian Church in April 1975.

The July 1979 cover of *The Australian Nurses Journal* showing Pixie Annat when she was President of the RANF with Bob Hawke, who was then President of the Australian Council of Trade Unions (ACTU).

She also recalled that after Dr Pye had retired, he had a stint as a patient at St Andrew's: 'I went down to see him and I walked in and said, "Hello, Dr Pye. How are you?" He said, "Sit down, my dear. Call me Aubrey". I was taken aback and I knew exactly what those kids, the young nurses, had felt like around Ken Jamieson. I just had great respect for Dr Pye and remembered his kindness to the nursing staff at the RBH. However, I did call him Aubrey after this.'

The eye unit was developed thanks to the $300,000 Simpson bequest, and the new Eye Wing included a new surgical block with 22 eye beds, 27 general surgical beds and three additional operating theatres. The new addition, officially opened in February 1974 by the Governor of Queensland, Air Marshall Sir Colin Hannah, was a boost for St Andrew's, adding to its reputation as a thriving small private hospital. Later that year, a new seven-bed intensive care unit and three-bed coronary care unit were opened, made possible once again by donations from loyal St Andrew's supporters.

From the outset, the Presbyterian founders of St Andrew's had wanted to build a nursing home as part of the hospital, and planning for this project began while the Eye Wing was still under development. The construction of the nursing home was fraught with problems, and when the building was only half-complete, the builder working on the project went into liquidation. At the same time, the hospital's X-ray Wing was being enlarged by the same builder, and because of all this building work, a number of surgical beds had been temporarily closed. It took time to appoint a new builder, complete all the work and readmit patients to the surgical beds, and these delays resulted in a big financial loss to the hospital in the mid-1970s.

'This created a lot of pressure on all of us involved in running St Andrew's. We all had to work together as a team and get through these difficult times. I was always very focused on making sure all the wards were running properly, and I relied on the charge sisters. When I think back, I remember so many marvellous people, like Sisters Mavis Currell, Alice Palmer, Marie Petersen, Peg Sullivan and Joy King (who also died very young), and later Jessie Bray and Jennifer West. They are just some of those who made a great contribution to the work and reputation of the hospital over the years.

'The operating theatres also made a huge contribution to the work of St Andrew's. The sister in charge for many years was Betty Buchanan; she was truly amazing and what she said was always taken as "gospel".'

Pixie always left her nursing staff to get on with the job, but one winter, when many people were away on sick leave, she called the theatres to offer to help: 'I thought perhaps I could help by trolleying a patient, for instance. When I phoned, a polite voice (not Betty's) said, "No, thank you, we're not that desperate!" I believe she thought I was about to invade the operating theatres proper.'

The St Andrew's Nursing Home was opened in August 1975 – once again by the ever-willing and good friend of the hospital, Governor of Queensland Air Marshall Sir Colin Hannah. The nursing home, funded in part from the proceeds of the sale of the Wavell Heights land, had been carefully planned. It not only provided 52 beds for chronically ill and aged patients, it also included a modern kitchen and cafeteria for St Andrew's War Memorial Hospital that improved how food was prepared and delivered. This helped St Andrew's cut domestic staff costs and also freed nurses from time-consuming meal serving tasks.

At the same time, a great deal of effort had been put into providing comfortable accommodation for the nurses at St Andrew's, who by 1970 resided in six nurses' quarters within the hospital or at nearby residences. These residences were the Avon and Arran on Gregory Terrace in Spring Hill, just across the road from the Brisbane Grammar School.

The ambitious building projects at St Andrew's from 1970 to 1975 had cost approximately $3 million, and the funds had come from grassroots fundraising – from the likes of Scottish Fairs and doorknock Field Days – as well as small and large donations from benefactors. The drive displayed by Dr Mayes and Dr Jamieson were also important in keeping the hospital on track as it planned for the future. Dr Jamieson, in particular, as chair of the Planning Committee, had stamped his thoughtful, creative approach on all of the new areas of the hospital, including the new nursing home. Dr Jamieson's untimely death in January 1976 came as a shock to the close-knit St Andrew's community. He had been responsible for introducing high standards of neurosurgical care at St Andrew's, as he had done earlier at the RBH. He had also personally overseen the design of St Andrew's new operating theatres and the intensive care and coronary care units in association with anaesthetist Professor Tess O'Rourke Brophy (later Cramond). It was he who had authored numerous papers and books on head trauma and had been instrumental in campaigning for Australian legislation imposing limits to drivers' blood-alcohol level, the wearing of helmets by motorcyclists and compulsory safety belts in motor vehicles.

For Pixie, Dr Ken Jamieson's death 'left an irreplaceable void'.

'Dr Jamieson was probably one of the world's best neurosurgeons, and he died at the age of 51 from heart failure. He said to me one day, "You know, the best day of my life will be when I can go to bed at 8.00 pm at night and wake up at 5.00 am". He was constantly being called out, attending to patients who had been involved in car or other accidents. He gave of himself unstintingly. The day he died was the afternoon before his daughter's wedding. Sister Noble, who was in charge of the neurosurgical theatre at the RBH, phoned and said to me, "Dr Jamieson has gone home early today". He'd gone home to mow the lawn – he had wanted to make sure everything was perfect, because the wedding reception was being held at the family home. So home he went to mow the lawn, and he collapsed doing this. About four days later, one of the specialists at St Andrew's said to me, "If you or I died tomorrow, the world wouldn't even blink. Ken Jamieson dies, and he's irreplaceable". And he was. He was quite extraordinary, not only in his field of medicine, but in the way he supported St Andrew's, including his concern for our nurses.'

Remembrance was always highly valued at St Andrew's. The hospital commemorated Australia's war dead. When a beloved nurse died, a scholarship fund was set up in her memory. After Dr Jamieson died, St Andrew's established a special fund to further postgraduate nursing education in his memory. Once again, Pixie backed the nurses' suggestion to set up this fund – they felt that it was a small gesture that would acknowledge his enormous contribution to the hospital he had helped establish.

Another vital part of St Andrew's was its ongoing connection to the Presbyterian Church, whose members had willed the hospital into life. In 1976, St Andrew's marked off another project that had been on the 'to do' list for many years when the chapel was opened by the first full-time chaplain, the Reverend David Henry. The commissioning service was held in the courtyard in the shade of a poinciana tree, presided over by the Reverend Richard Diffin, moderator of the Brisbane Presbytery. In a little touch that was typical of how St Andrew's tried to include people, the hospital's cook since its first days, Miss Annie Rushton, was invited to accompany the chaplain into the chapel for the dedication. Miss Rushton was an institution at the hospital, and a great favourite of Pixie's.

'Her glasses were always covered in flour, and so every morning after breakfast I would clean them for her. She seldom got upset, but I do remember an occasion when we were in the old kitchen where the chapel would later be built. We were discussing the problem of the limited space in the cold room and before our eyes, a large pile of sliced beetroot that had been resting on top of a milk can slipped into the milk. She burst into tears.

'Annie once asked me for the names of the six sickest patients who could still eat. She decided to personally visit them and take their orders for lunch and dinner that day; she made sure that each of them got their specially requested meals. Those patients commented the next day on just how much they appreciated what Annie had done for them.'

Catering at St Andrew's was supported by the Auxiliary, whose members served for many years at the 'Kiosk' coffee shop, built in the hospital courtyard in 1978. Ellie, who had joined the Auxiliary on returning to the Brisbane area in 1975, was a popular volunteer at the Kiosk. Each Friday at 4.30 am, she would set off from her home on Bribie Island, drive to Caboolture Station, catch the train to Central Station and be at St Andrew's in time to open the Kiosk by 7.00 am. Quite often in the morning, she would still be turning on the urns and performing other opening rituals when she would hear a tapping on the shutters. She would go out and say, 'Give me five minutes, please', and find a family already waiting, often having driven several hours from a country area to come to St Andrew's. Pixie always made a point of seeing Ellie when she came to St Andrew's, and her Friday mornings began with a drive to Central Station to collect her sister.

As busy as she was, Pixie also continued her outside interests. She and Ellie, like their parents, loved cricket, and the sisters were members of the Gabba – the Brisbane Cricket Ground in Woolloongabba – for more than 20 years. They regularly attended Sheffield Shield cricket matches in the members' section, sitting in the same seats, and were something of an institution, always bringing their own morning tea complete with bone china tea cups. 'We used to hear people say, "I wonder what the twins have brought for morning tea today?" I remember sitting up there for evening matches, and the lights would come on and we'd look at each other and I'd say, "We wouldn't call the Queen our aunt now, would we?"' Pixie also had a 'very special gentleman friend', Ron Glenney, who was her partner at many balls, dances and dinners, and other social events.

She worked on Saturday mornings then went home for the weekend to her house where her parents lived, and as they aged she tended to them with great love and care. In 1976, Pixie managed to take them on a holiday to New Zealand. The following year, 1977, they both moved to the St Andrew's Nursing Home. Jim Annat died later that year at the age of 86, while Madoline died in 1980 at 85 years of age. Losing her parents resulted in a long grieving process for Pixie.

Looking back, Pixie commented: 'Dad was a retiring sort of person – he never drew attention to himself and seldom mentioned his commendable war record from World War I during which he was awarded a military medal. He had a great sense of humour and was a very good family man. Mother was a highly respected nurse who kept in touch with many of her nurse friends through committees like the Centaur Memorial Fund Committee. They were both strong characters. Ellie related more to Father and of course I had the nursing experience in common with Mother.'

In 1978, the St Andrew's board appointed Pixie as hospital administrator, later called CEO. This was a significant achievement at a time when women were still routinely overlooked for advancement. In the same year, the Australian Council on Healthcare Standards, responsible for accreditation of hospitals, appointed Pixie as a surveyor, and it was the first time a private hospital was represented on the council. The role involved assessing hospitals' compliance with healthcare standards, and she travelled widely as part of a three-person surveyor team. This work widened her appreciation of the intricacies of health care at a national level. All these responsibilities represented an almost impossible workload – her commitment to St Andrew's alone was daunting.

'It was at least a 16-hour-a-day job. It had to be your life, because there was no-one else to do it. I used to be down on duty by six in the morning and I would finish at eleven o'clock at night, and that was five days a week. On Saturday morning, I'd take myself into the boardroom, close the door and wouldn't answer the phone, so I could catch up on all the things that had happened during the week. I used to think sometimes that people thought it was a bit unusual that a woman was sitting up in the top possie at the hospital. It was unusual, I suppose, but it was a job to me and it meant a lot because I understood where the nurses were coming from, and I loved patient care.'

While St Andrew's was her primary focus, Pixie's extracurricular RANF activities came a close second. Having served as president of the RANF Queensland Branch from 1967 to 1969, she spent the 1970s as a national leader of the RANF, serving as vice-president from 1971 to 1975 and president until 1979. At the same time, she continued to serve on the council of the RANF Queensland and was the RANF's representative when International Council of Nurses meetings were held. Improved education for nurses remained a priority, and she was a member of the RANF Queensland Branch Committee of Enquiry into nursing set up in 1971. The enquiry panel included academics from the University of Queensland Medical School as well as several nurse representatives.

'For a long time we met in secret because the Minister for Health, Doug Tooth, and his bureaucrats would not have approved. We used to call it the "007 committee" because it was such a secret.' The RANF provided a detailed report to the Queensland government, recommending that serious consideration be given to shifting nurse education to colleges of advanced education, and out of hospitals, but the report failed to resonate with the government.

'Doug Tooth was always a very difficult man to deal with. He had no idea about nursing issues. I met with him and Violet Hall, who was the president of the RANF, on his very first day as minister in the mid-1960s. He met us and had three of his bureaucrats sitting there, and one of them took down every word that was said. At one stage in the discussion, Violet disagreed with him on a point. He looked at her and said, "I would like to remind you, Mrs Hall, that you are speaking to a Minister of the Crown". That was his first day in office.'

From 1976, Pixie served on another RANF advanced education committee on nurse education to investigate and make recommendations on a future standard for nursing. In this capacity, she and her colleagues attended countless meetings with Queensland and federal government agencies. The RANF's frustration with political decisions that were made about nursing and nurse training was summed up in a resolution carried at a RANF Queensland Branch meeting in 1976, which stated: '... the members deplore the secrecy with which certain policy decisions on health care are made at both Federal and State levels and [wish] this be known to the Federal and State Ministers for Health'.

As the 1970s progressed, however, it was not just education issues but also industrial relations that often vexed Pixie and her RANF colleagues.

Since the 1950s, most RANF state organisations consisted of two sections: one focused on professional and education issues, and the other, an 'employee section' dedicated to industrial relations and state government award issues. Ideological tensions would continue to bubble away between RANF leaders like Pixie, who were cautious about aligning the RANF with the trade union movement, and other emerging figures in nurse politics, some of whom worked for the employee sections and favoured a more militant stance. By 1976, two separate legal entities were created – the RANF Queensland Branch and the RANF Queensland Branch Union of Employees. It would take another six years before a formal split between these two organisations occurred.

For the majority of Pixie's working life as a nurse, nurse leader and hospital manager, from 1957 until 1989, conservative governments were in power in Queensland. While politically she was a Liberal Party voter, she had shown herself quite prepared to take an independent stance in her dealings with Health Ministers and the 'bureaucrats' in the Health Department. She would remain unafraid to speak her mind when she thought the occasion warranted it, sometimes taking steps that would surprise her colleagues.

'Some of the most interesting years of my life were when I was federal president of the RANF. They were very formative years. It was a time when there was a lot of industrial disharmony, not in nursing but in industrial relations in general. These non-medically oriented unions wanted to take over the RANF because we had the members, but we just wouldn't go along with it. It got so bad that I had to approach Bob Hawke, who was President of the Australian Council of Trade Unions (ACTU). I wasn't a supporter of the Labor Party, but when I met him in Melbourne in 1978 I said we would join the ACTU if we didn't have to go on sympathy strike. He looked at me and said, "If you come into the ACTU, we will respect that view". And I knew he meant what he said. Well, my friends up here in Queensland couldn't believe it when I came back and wrote to all the members of the RANF and informed them of this alliance. We joined for protection because we faced being taken over and threatened.'

The cover of *The Australian Nurses Journal* of July 1979 featured a photograph of Pixie, then outgoing president of the RANF, and Bob Hawke under the headline, 'Presidents Meet'. The article explained that the RANF Federal Council had invited Bob Hawke 'to chew the fat – as well as a sandwich', during a break at the annual council meeting.

It was not just industrial relations that consumed Pixie's time during her presidency of the RANF. Her responsibilities extended to council meetings and numerous subcommittees, annual conferences, speaking engagements, reports and keeping track of finances. She had a tendency to never say no when volunteers were needed for a particular cause or activity. It meant she was always 'busy', and this became a way of life.

Pixie also attended many International Council of Nurses meetings, including travelling to California in 1974 and Tokyo in 1977. This broadened her appreciation of the improvements being made to nurse education around the world and reinforced her view that Australia was lagging behind in providing tertiary education for nurses.

Pixie, as president of the RANF, was invited to serve on a federal government committee set up in 1977 to investigate nurse education, chaired by Adelaide pathologist Dr Sidney Sax. She recalled travelling frequently to meetings as part of the committee's deliberations. The Sax Report into nursing education was released in 1978 and recommended that hospital-based education of nurses continue to be provided largely by hospitals rather than colleges – because this was a more cost-effective option for the government.

The release of the report coincided with the annual national conference of the College of Nursing Australia (CNA) in Adelaide, which Pixie attended, and delegates were so incensed by Dr Sax's recommendations that they decided to stage a protest march down Rundle Street in Adelaide.

'The executive of the CNA decided on this march down Rundle Street, and we marched along with Baroness Jean MacFarlane, who was the first female nursing professor in England, and she was in Adelaide to attend the CNA meeting. So we went four abreast down Rundle Street, including the nuns, which was quite extraordinary. I was in the fourth row from the front and suddenly this big police motorcycle came up to us and this policeman asked us, "What are you marching for? You look pretty well-heeled!" We told him we weren't marching for money, we were marching for nurse education. He said, "Well, let's tell 'em!" And he revved his engine and said, "We're marching for nursing education!" I thought the professor was going to fall over, she'd never seen such a thing in her life. When we got to Minister [Neal] Blewett's office, he wasn't there, of course, and some of the marchers set fire to the report and placed it in a bed pan. We were front-page news all over the country. When I got back to St Andrew's I bumped into one of the board members, and he asked me if I had been involved in the business in Adelaide where the nurses had burnt the Sax Report. And I said, "Yes, I was. I was in the fourth line, and I don't regret it".

'Dr Sax did not like nurses. When I served on this committee, there were only two nurse representatives: myself, as federal president of the RANF, and Ronnie Henlon, who was secretary of the New South Wales Nurses' Association. She was a tough cookie, too, and at this one particular meeting Dr Sax made sure we weren't allowed to sit next to each other. Dr Sax was chairing this meeting, and I had said to him, "I have a particular interest in the care of the aged because I think they have been badly neglected". He said, "Now ladies and gentlemen, Miss Annat would like to talk to you", and he gestured as if he was playing a violin, "about aged care". I think the people around the table were quite stunned. I looked directly at him and said, "If you have quite finished Dr Sax, I indeed do have something to say about aged care", and I took my time to have my say. That was the kind of thing we had to put up with. I said to Mary Patten, who was secretary of the RANF, that this committee was "a damn waste of time, just one for the bureaucrats to hide behind. So I'm not going back". And I never did.'

The time and effort nurse leaders like Pixie and many others gave in attempting to influence the direction of nursing education ran into thousands of hours. Just as at the federal level the RANF and other nurse representatives were pushing for nurse education to move from hospitals to tertiary institutions, so at a state level they were determined to lobby for nurse education to be provided by advanced colleges.

Pixie felt that over the years relationships improved between the RANF and the Queensland government, thanks in part to the constructive approach taken by the Minister for Health, Dr Llew Edwards: 'He phoned me once and asked me whether I had heard from the department that training would be moving into colleges of advanced education. Of course, I hadn't heard. He said, "You will, because it is government policy". And eventually it did. Dr Edwards became one of our greatest supporters in having nursing education transferred to tertiary institutions.'

As fellow nurse managers, Pixie would often consult with the Mater's Sister Angela Mary and with Elizabeth Ann Abell, who was matron – later called nursing superintendent – at the RBH, particularly through the RANF Queensland Branch's Nursing Administration Section to which all three belonged. The same determination to support her fellow nurses saw Pixie support Miss Abell when in 1978 the North Brisbane Hospitals Board demoted her from the position of nursing superintendent of the RBH to that of nursing supervisor of the Royal Women's Hospital. The RANF, including Pixie and the entire Queensland and national executives, supported her appeal to the Supreme Court against her demotion. Nurses at the RBH rallied around her, wearing civilian clothing or black armbands on their white uniforms to show their support. She was recognised as a woman who had made huge strides for nurses at the hospital, including opening the nurse training to male students, encouraging further education for nurses and also fighting for married women to remain on the staff. She was ultimately reinstated in 1979 and later appointed chief nursing officer of the Queensland Department of Health – a vindication widely celebrated by nurses.

As the 1970s drew to a close, St Andrew's continued to chalk up some significant firsts, including the opening of a neurosensory unit in March 1979. For a private hospital like St Andrew's, it was important to continue to break new ground. The health system for patients in Queensland was being transformed by medical innovations. Change at St Andrew's and other private hospitals was mirrored by many improvements for patients at the large state hospitals – all the while the inadequate training of and remuneration for nurses both in Queensland and the rest of Australia remained unresolved.

## Chapter 7

# Challenges and Triumphs

## 1980–1984

The 1980s was a decade that would bring fresh challenges for Pixie, both in her role as CEO of St Andrew's and as a nursing leader in Australia. There were some difficult days ahead, but she tackled the issues as she saw them in her customary no-nonsense way.

In many respects, Brisbane was on the cusp of change: the Commonwealth Games in 1982 and the successful staging of Expo in 1988 transformed the sleepy city in the eyes of residents and visitors alike. It was a decade that also saw conflict, often played out in street protests as demonstrators who usually gathered for marches at King George Square protested over issues as diverse as Aboriginal land rights, labour laws and even the right to protest over the aggressive tactics employed by the Joh Bjelke-Petersen government to quash opposition. Nurses and student nurses, who were members of the RANF, were also involved in many rallies in the 1970s and early 1980s, either at King George Square or the Roma Street Forum. Other parts of the country also experienced a wave of industrial disputes: Victoria in particular was the scene of drawn-out threats of strike action and protests by nurses who were becoming increasingly vocal on issues such as nurse shortages, wages and working conditions.

The 1980s was also the last decade of hospital-based training for nurses in Australia – in spite of the Sax Report, change was on the way as more tertiary institutions, including the Queensland Institute of Technology, began to offer undergraduate diplomas, and later degrees, for nurses.

The St Andrew's School of Nursing accepted its final intake of students in the mid-1980s, but the decade began on a bright note with a record 34 students graduating in March 1980. The graduation ceremony that year was held in the garden at St Andrew's, instead of, as was usually the custom, in one of the city's beautiful Presbyterian churches. The guest speaker at the graduation ceremony was Governor of Queensland Sir James Ramsay, who paid tribute to the high standard of nurse training at St Andrew's, exemplified by the achievement of graduate Robyn Webster who had been placed first in the 1979 State Nursing Examination. Pixie felt this reflected the high calibre of nurses who trained at St Andrew's, and she believed that it proved that when nurses and doctors worked together, they could achieve extraordinary things.

'I always witnessed the best results when we worked at the hospital as a team. Our principal nurse educators, Joan Coyer and later Dell Tidey, were excellent, and they were supported by a number of other very good nurse educators and our doctors. There was a genuine tradition of caring – our doctors always gave lectures at no cost to the hospital – they really were concerned, not just about their patients but about St Andrew's, and that included helping educate the students.'

Another central character in the lives of nurses at St Andrew's during this time was Miss Beatrice Lemon, who had assumed the role of nursing superintendent after Pixie became CEO. She served at the hospital for 29 years.

'Lemon by name and lemon by nature' was how Miss Lemon self-deprecatingly styled herself, and while she was rather formidable and tough on the nurses at times, she was also known to be a stout defender of, and protective towards, the nurses. Pixie regarded Miss Lemon as an excellent nurse and very caring at heart, even though the young student nurses did not always know quite how to take her.

'She was particularly kind to some of our older patients who might have fallen on hard times. If they didn't have proper attire, she would produce a nightie and bed jacket for them ... She would also sometimes jokingly ask the students whether they had warm underclothing on in winter, and if they said they "no", she would say, "When you go off duty, write 500 times, 'I must wear warm underwear in winter.'" One lass took Miss Lemon at her word and presented her with 500 lines the next day!

'Bea Lemon was a woman of great physical stature, very smart; she looked more like the matron than I did. She greeted me every morning, saying, "Good morning, Miss Annex." On one occasion she was late for a meeting that was being held in the boardroom in the administration building, so I sent one of the nurses to find out where she was. She was in the nurses' quarters one floor up and was still in the shower – there had been some confusion about the time of the meeting – and she was quite taken aback when this nurse said to her, "That's all right, Miss Lemon, come as you are".'

As complex as Pixie's role became, the nurses were always central to her thinking when it came to patient care.

'I remember right from when I started nursing the pleasure I took in making a patient feel comfortable. And I'd tell the student nurses at St Andrew's that if you can really attend to what a patient needs, not just clinically, but also making them comfortable, fixing their bed up and getting them ready to sleep at night, and when they look up and purr at you, you've achieved something. That might not be a fashionable thing to say these days, but that's how it was.'

The approach to nursing at St Andrew's was, of course, comprehensive; under Pixie and Bea's leadership, and together with the School of Nursing, St Andrew's adopted a formal 'Philosophy of Nursing Service' in the 1970s. It was a companion document to a wider 'Philosophy' for the entire hospital. The nursing 'Philosophy', similar in many respects to 'nursing codes' colleagues in state hospitals had adopted, began with a declaration that:

'The patient is recognised as the reason for the presence of the nurse at the workplace. Standards of patient care and safety must take priority over all other considerations. Race, creed, colour or social status shall not influence standards of care given to patients … The comfort and well being of patients and their loved ones and the creation of a safe and pleasant environment must be the prime consideration of all nursing staff.'

Under Bea Lemon and Pixie Annat's direction, St Andrew's adopted 'team nursing', which meant that a team of professionals was responsible for all aspects of a particular group of patients' care.

'Some of the doctors were not keen on "team nursing". We had one doctor on staff, Dr John Phillips, who was highly respected, and he knew the doctors were getting bitchy about this "team nursing" business. I happened to be with him in a ward and we looked up and there were about seven of the doctors standing near a nurses' station, all complaining about this. And John walked up and looked at one of the charts and said to the sister on duty, "Hello, Sister, how are you? Who is my team leader today?" And I never heard another complaint about this from the doctors.'

This 'Philosophy', a simple one-page document, also set out things like the principles behind education programs at St Andrew's, how nurses were expected to work with their hospital colleagues, and the importance of conducting regular reviews of nursing policies, procedures and standards of practice.

Standards of practice at St Andrew's were put to the test in a very real way when a fire broke out in the hospital on the night of 5 March 1981. It certainly was a night of high drama.

Earlier that evening, the RANF Queensland Branch Union of Employees had called a meeting at the nearby Teachers' Building on Boundary Street in Spring Hill, and Pixie and many of her friends in the RANF attended as 'ordinary members'. At the heart of the issue at this time was a schism between two leadership factions – one represented by longstanding RANF Queensland Branch leaders like Pixie who also belonged to the Nursing Administration Section of RANF Queensland, and the other group whose power base was the RANF Queensland Branch Union of Employees, who were determined to draw the tens of thousands of Queensland nurses under their wing. Pixie has vivid recollections about the events of that night:

'I went down from St Andrew's to go to this special meeting, and as I walked across the road to enter the building, this great big man stood in front of me. I said, "Excuse me" and he didn't move, and I thought, "Don't say I'm going to die on Boundary Street", because these funny sorts of threats had been coming through to me for some time. He said, "You could be in physical danger tonight and I am here to see that you don't get hurt". He told me Monica Rochford, who was a nurse at the Greenslopes Hospital, which was the Repatriation Hospital in those days, had sent for him because she had been worried about me. This man was about six foot six, and had a large pair of shoulders on him. He looked like an ex-policeman. He said, "You go into the meeting and I will be here for you when you come out, and I'll take you up to St Andrew's". And he did just that.

'It was an awful meeting. The vice-president passed some remark and I indicated that I wanted to speak. He sent a fellow with a microphone, a male nurse, to me and he pushed the microphone right towards my mouth as I was trying to speak. I said what I wanted to say, and I got a clap from around the room. There were hundreds of nurses there. I thought, "I've had enough of this", I'd said my piece and I got up and left.

'As I left the building, there was my new "friend" waiting for me, and he walked me back to St Andrew's. And as we were walking up the hill, I saw the assistant director of nursing, Ivy Trede, come running across the front doctor's car park, and I said, "What's wrong?" She said, "There's a fire".'

A fire had broken out in the central sterilising department's stores area at 10.30 pm, triggering the fire alarm. The fire brigade arrived within minutes and quickly extinguished the blaze as night staff and other helpers began evacuating patients to five patient location areas outside. At least 20 nurses from other hospitals, who had attended the RANF meeting in Boundary Street earlier in the evening, also came to lend a hand with patients.

'We'd had a lot of fire drills, and it was clear on everyone's timesheet for the week what their role was in the event of an emergency, but we were still hugely relieved that no-one was injured. We set people up under the trees, on chairs, and so on, and then the police arrived. Nothing was ever proved, but police had their suspicions. The only laugh I got was later in the night when I went up to one elderly lady sitting under the trees in the car park, and I said, "Are you alright?" She looked at me, and she had a real English accent and replied, "Cor, love, it's like being back in the Blitz!"'

In the early hours of the next morning, once the smoke had cleared, most patients, except those closest to the sterilising department, were returned to their beds, carried in by nurses and firemen. Patients nearer to where the fire had started were relocated to other wards. In the days that followed, St Andrew's was overwhelmed by offers of help from many other Brisbane hospitals. The Holy Spirit Hospital and The Wesley Hospital sent 'theatre bundles' and other disposable items to St Andrew's, and phone calls of support continued for days. The fire, disruptive and disturbing as it was, was a demonstration of how staff came together in difficult circumstances. Board chairman Dr Alex Mayes wrote an open letter to all staff thanking them for 'the magnificent work and calm discipline'. Pixie also made a point of writing to every hospital's nursing superintendent or administrator, commending nurses who had been at the RANF meeting that evening and had come up to St Andrew's to help. She was particularly grateful to receive a call from the Catholic Archbishop of Brisbane, Francis Roberts Rush, to ask if St Andrew's needed any help.

The conflict between the RANF Queensland Branch and the RANF Queensland Branch Union of Employees came to a head in early 1982 after state council elections resulted in victory for the latter faction. It brought about a 'physical separation' of the two organisations and a rather perplexing situation for nurses, who were represented at the state level by the union and at a national level by the branch. The RANF Queensland Branch employees were ejected from the RANF offices and most monies reverted to the union. This created a financial crisis for the branch, which had to find alternative accommodation, reorganise its office and issue separate bills to the 30,000 Queensland RANF members – who had already paid their annual fees to the union.

This situation caused great heartache – Pixie's RANF files from that period, which she meticulously maintained, were labelled in bold red letters as 'DIFFICULT YEARS'. But it was during this period that she also formed many of her enduring friendships – with colleagues like Margaret (Meg) Gagen. Meg's account of how she had first encountered her friend at St Andrew's in the late 1970s is another typical tale about Pixie.

Meg had begun nurse training in 1956 at Greenslopes Hospital, but left in 1959 when she married. Like many women who married and had children, she found it difficult to re-enter nursing with incomplete qualifications. She had heard of another 'mature nurse', a mother of five, who had completed her training at St Andrew's, and so in September 1967 Meg went to see Pixie. Pixie told her that the Nurses' Registration Board on which she served was dominated by doctors and that they 'weren't very keen about married women finishing their training'. Pixie said to Meg: 'If I take this to the board and fight this case, I want a commitment from you that you'll finish your training.' Meg readily agreed. She completed her training at St Andrew's in 1969, then undertook training as a midwife and in child health, and was later employed at the RANF Queensland office. She lost her job when she was 'booted out' of the RANF Spring Hill office after the split with the union in 1982 and was later employed as the secretary of the RANF Queensland Branch.

Along with other colleagues like Mary Abbot and Beth Johnstone, this group steered the RANF Queensland Branch in working on the 'professional side of nursing'. They believed that the union's focus on industrial relations 'was only half of what it was about for nurses'. According to Mary, Pixie was instrumental in helping introduce a generation of Queensland nursing leaders to nursing colleagues from abroad, most of whom were part of the International Council of Nurses, and this helped provide nurses with '... a serious sense of our place in the world. Pixie had a serious sense of commitment to nursing itself and also to our nursing colleagues – the care and education of nurses.'

Throughout the 1980s, this RANF group continued to meet with government bodies and educational institutions to try to ensure nurses' interests were represented as training moved progressively from hospitals to advanced colleges of education. Pixie's contacts helped ensure their voices were heard, particularly in Queensland – and her confidence and enthusiasm were infectious. If a delegation of nurse representatives wanted to meet with the

Australian Medical Association, for example, Pixie had the relationships with doctors 'to make this happen'. She had developed skills and insights and was generous about sharing her knowledge with her nurse colleagues. For Mary, Pixie was a 'role model ... She wasn't a teacher and I wasn't either, but we knew how important it was to be nurturing and caring for our students. Pixie always demonstrated that in spades.'

By 1983, Pixie had regained her equilibrium after a tough time. This was a significant year for St Andrew's as it celebrated its 25th anniversary, its Silver Jubilee. Activities to mark the celebration were diverse: a three-day health technology conference in the western Brisbane suburb of Bardon, a dinner dance at the Crest Hotel in the city, a photographic display of the hospital's history, an arts and crafts exhibition at the St Andrew's School of Nursing, a church service in the hospital's garden courtyard and, for good measure, a barbecue for staff. A large Silver Jubilee Planning Committee, headed by Pixie, managed this ambitious program.

Among the sessions at the Silver Jubilee conference entitled 'Technology in Hospitals – The Next 25 Years' was a panel discussion called 'Human Infertility – Is In-Vitro Fertilisation the Answer?' It might have come as a surprise to people who did not know Pixie well that she was so interested in, and supportive of, IVF. Only five years after the birth of the UK 'test tube baby', Louise Brown, a small IVF unit was established at St Andrew's – when it was still a controversial and untested technology.

'The board nearly died when I suggested we start IVF – I had been approached by Dr John Hennessy [co-founder of the Queensland Fertility Group]. You would have thought I was suggesting we run a brothel. They looked at me and said, "What?" I said, "It's for people who can't have a family by the natural method". They sent me down to Melbourne and I looked at the facilities operating there, and I persuaded them that it was all above board.'

During the early 1980s, the St Andrew's board began considering improved facilities for a host of hospital services, including IVF, and new cardiac and nuclear medicine departments. They realised the hospital needed to modernise and expand in order to survive financially.

The shift in thinking about the future of the hospital coincided with the passing of the guard at St Andrew's: the board chairman, Dr Mayes, died in St Andrew's War Memorial Hospital in February 1983 at the age of eighty-one. The *St Andrew's Messenger* celebrated his life with a front-page story entitled 'One Man and His Community', noting that 'dear to his heart were the traditions, the manners and the culture of Scotland', and that at the time of his death he was chairman of the Society of St Andrew of Scotland (Queensland) and had served for many years as president of the Caledonian Society. Pixie greatly admired him:

'Dr Mayes was a man of great vision and courage, generous of spirit and a Scot to his bootstrap. He visited the hospital every day to see patients and any staff who were sick. During the week he wore a dark suit and bow tie, and at weekends, a sports jacket and trousers and a long Society of St Andrew of Scotland tie. At formal occasions, he naturally wore his kilt and dinner jacket.'

Pixie missed him very much. In addition to their devotion to St Andrew's, the pair shared their love of cricket – Dr Mayes had been a member of the first Queensland Sheffield Shield team in the 1920s. Almost every morning, Dr Mayes would have an early morning cup of tea with Pixie to discuss the hospital, and they often analysed whatever cricket match happened to be in progress. They would also discuss any Scottish social events that were coming up at St Andrew's, and often haggis was on the menu. For many years, Dr Mayes personally prepared the haggis for dinners and brought it to St Andrew's where Pixie left it 'cooking' on her stove top in her flat. 'You could smell the haggis cooking for days afterwards. Bea Lemon used to say, "Is that the damn haggis again?"'

Pixie and Dr Mayes had also discussed at length future plans for St Andrew's, and this included a plan for an expanded hospital and on-site specialist rooms. The new chairman, orthopaedic surgeon Dr William (Bill) Crawford, who was the son of inaugural board chairman Dr Harold Crawford, quickly ramped up the proposals to expand the hospital. Among the changes Bill Crawford oversaw was an improved X-ray department. He also supported a major new hospital development, known as 'the Dr Alex Mayes Memorial Project'.

From 1984 to 1986, St Andrew's was once again a hive of activity as construction commenced for, among other things, five levels of car parking, several new floors of hospital wards, three additional operating theatres and a new laundry. The decision to proceed with this project came with considerable financial risk – the budget for the development was $17 million, a very large sum of money in those days, and this was a time of high inflation and soaring interest rates. Within a few years, the debt was to rise to $22 million. The hospital survived, thanks to good board oversight but also because money from donors helped bridge the financial gap. Fundraising activity had always been at the heart and soul of St Andrew's, and in Pixie's final decade as CEO, her exceptional ability to help attract donations was to make an enormous difference to the future of the hospital.

## Chapter 8

# A Loyal CEO Says Farewell

### 1985–1992

In 1985, St Andrew's War Memorial Hospital announced that it was to become the first private hospital in Queensland to offer open-heart surgery. This was significant news, and many doctors privately wondered whether the hospital was 'punching above its weight'. Pixie was convinced that St Andrew's was more than up to the challenge.

'Some of the medical staff discussed with me the proposal to set up a cardiac unit – first a diagnostic cardiac catheter laboratory, to be followed by cardiac surgery. And I agreed because we had a lot of cardiac patients coming in for general care and who were waiting for public hospital heart surgery. So we set about raising the money for a new unit, and this was a huge undertaking.

'A member of the fundraising staff said to me, "Have you met Barry Paul? He's the CEO of Kern Corporation. He's one of the nicest men, and he can get blood out of a stone". And that was exactly what we needed, blood out of a stone. So I made an appointment to see him, he was down at the bottom of Eagle Street in the city. I rang his secretary and said I wanted to talk to Mr Paul about our hospital. So this young man came out, he couldn't have been any more than 40 at the time. He said, "What can I do for you?" I said, "Well, I told the board that I wanted to set up a cardiac unit at St Andrew's and they said we needed $2 million to do it". Barry said to me, "I'll help you do it. I'll come up to the hospital every second Friday. I'll give you the names of the people to invite, and I'll host the lunches with you". During this time of intense fundraising, I got to know Barry and his wife, Stephanie, very well. They were both marvellous people.

'Within a little over 12 months, we had raised the $2 million. And Barry helped us reach this goal. He would sit at the head of the table at the lunches and say to the guests, "Now, you know you are here because I invited you to this luncheon today. We are going to set up a cardiac unit at St Andrew's, and many of us will be in it before we die. I've given $70,000, now what are you prepared to give?" We held lunches almost every second Friday, and in that way we raised a lot of the money we needed. Sadly, Barry also died early and didn't see the full fruits of his labour.'

Pixie believed that to be successful with fundraising you had to find the people with the right contacts and offer donors a 'bricks and mortar' vision: 'One of the people who gave quite a lot of money to our eye unit at St Andrew's once said to me that they donated to us "because you and Dr Crawford and some other members of the board work so damn hard". They liked to see evidence of where the money was being spent.'

Other donors whom Pixie befriended included Clem Jones, former Lord Mayor of Brisbane: 'Clem Jones was a big supporter of ours, and he used to run golf days for us. The first day he came to a morning tea at our boardroom, I asked him if I could call him "Clem", because he had always been Mr Jones to me. He said, "You can call me Clem if I can call you Pixie." I said, "You can call me whatever you like as long as you help me raise some money", and he said, "The first thing we'll do is to have a golf day", and they were very successful.'

The idea of setting up a private heart service at St Andrew's was driven by specialists based at the public Prince Charles Hospital, who saw it as a way of providing desperately needed additional heart disease diagnosis and cardiac surgery in Queensland: 'Dr Michael Gardner was a cardiac surgeon at Prince Charles, and he had spoken to board chair Bill Crawford and myself about the need for a private cardiac unit as a way of alleviating the pressure on the public system and creating a much-needed private facility.'

St Andrew's embraced the idea and a strategic plan was developed. The initial specialist team consisted of Prince Charles Hospital cardiac surgeons Dr Michael Gardner, Dr Greg Stafford and Dr Mark O'Brien, and cardiologists Dr David Pritchard and Dr Roger Wilkinson. The plan was to initially commence cardiac catheterisation in 1984 followed by open-heart surgery within a year, depending on the success of the catheter lab.

The cardiac catheter lab was an immediate hit and in high demand from patients eager for early diagnosis of heart conditions. The next step was to offer open-heart surgery, and this service commenced at St Andrew's in 1985: 'It was truly historic – we had key surgeons from the Prince Charles behind us, and it was not long before more cardiologists joined us. Dr Jim Cameron became the leader of the cardiologists undertaking cardiac catheterisations at St Andrew's.'

Support from the medical specialists was critical. But Pixie knew St Andrew's needed to build its nursing capability, so she sent Sister Pat Kinghorn to the Seventh Day Adventist hospital in Sydney for training: 'The hospital had a well-established cardiac surgical department. I was a friend of the matron and she was happy to have Pat for a month down there. When Pat came back, I contacted the matron and offered to remunerate the hospital and she said, "There is no payment necessary, it was a pleasure to help". That's how it was, people were so good.'

Dr Rosemary Hay, an intensive care unit doctor who worked closely with Pixie, recalled the teamwork involved with the new undertaking:

'St Andrew's had the support of the cardiologists, cardiac surgeons and theatre staff from Prince Charles. The Prince Charles nurses would come back and forth to assist in theatre. It was an informal arrangement and Pixie allowed it to happen. Later on, St Andrew's own nurses gained the experience they needed to fully staff the theatres.

'So virtually, St Andrew's got an annex of a highly respected open-heart unit, thanks to the experience and support of the Prince Charles team. The second year the service took off, and in 1986 and 1987 specialists at St Andrew's performed around 730 procedures – and after that units at other hospitals started to open up, but we maintained very high numbers of surgeries with excellent results for years to come.'

Rosemary described the open-heart surgery from that era as '… pioneering. Everyone worked together. The camaraderie was fantastic. We were all on the same page and it was a very stimulating atmosphere to work in.'

With the introduction of cardiac services at St Andrew's, another important change was the employment of full-time doctors. This was managed by Dr Grant Cameron, who served on the hospital board.

Pixie said: 'St Andrew's was the first private hospital in Queensland to employ full-time, 24-hour, seven-day-a-week medical staff, and this became the standard for quality care in private hospitals managing major surgery. Michael Gardner and our other specialists made it clear that we needed full-time doctors to properly provide cardiac care. We believed nursing staff should not have to take full responsibility for care of these patients, particularly at night when doctors might be called, and that medical care provided by doctors should be available on tap. The 24-hour St Andrew's Medical Service worked very well, and I think the visiting specialists appreciated that our doctors were always available.'

Rosemary's introduction to St Andrew's was at a job interview with Pixie: 'I didn't know her, but everyone else seemed to know her – and I'll never forget that during our meeting she offered me a whisky. Pixie was fantastic. She was never a downtrodden handmaiden to the doctors – she was a driving force. She was part of a team at St Andrew's that could see ahead, and so the next thing they started planning were doctors' rooms across the road from St Andrew's, and that became St Andrew's Place.'

Rosemary worked with Pixie for eight years and got to know her very well: 'You would always hear the click, click, click down the corridors if Pixie was coming along. And then you'd hear a pause. Usually that was because she was picking up a piece of paper or litter. She would never walk past a piece of untidiness in the corridors – she would stop and pick it up herself. And she always dined in the staff dining room at the same table; and usually at the same time, she would be having a meeting with someone. Everyone would approach her as they walked out of the cafe. I used to see the cleaning ladies stop and have a little bit of a whinge to her, and I would hear her say, "Really? I'll look into it straight away". I didn't know if she ever did, but it was a fantastic form of management. They'd walk out with a smile on their faces. She'd have these huge functions and there was usually a big bunch of flowers for the kitchen staff, she was very personal in her approach.'

Considering the 'domestic staff' had always been important to Pixie. She recalled an annual St Andrew's dinner in the city where actress Diane Cilento, daughter of the famous medical couple Sir Raphael and Lady Phyllis Cilento, was the guest speaker for the evening: 'After Diane arrived, these other stretch limousines pulled up to drop off guests. Diane asked me, "Who are they?" I said, "They're the domestic staff". She said, "Evidence of good morale in a hospital". It was true. They were marvellous, those domestics.'

From her early years at St Andrew's until her final year as CEO in 1992, those who worked with Pixie recalled a woman with imperfections like everyone else, but above all a woman who was totally committed to her staff. She particularly tried to find time to listen to what nurses thought. It had become her habit in her role as director of nursing to have an 'open door' to anyone who wanted to speak to her.

'In my 13 years as director of nursing, every afternoon from 3.00 pm to 4.00 pm was the staff's time. Anyone could come up to my office, they just needed to ring my secretary to say they wanted to see me. They'd spend about ten minutes with me, and if it was necessary, it would be longer. My friend Helen Banff, who was matron of The Wesley Hospital, did the same sort of thing. Because people had to be listened to.'

Jennifer West, a nurse who was appointed the supervisor of many of St Andrew's services including the intensive care unit in 1990, recalled Pixie's loyalty to her staff: 'She used to advocate that without good staff you've got nothing. She had a strong philosophy about people and she used to say, "When you've got good doctors, and good nursing staff, you've got happy patients and you've got people doing well".'

Over the years of expansion at St Andrew's, Pixie made a habit of consulting the senior nurses when planning the new areas of the hospital: 'I would say to the board, "When we get the architect's plans, do you mind if I get the director of nursing and the charge sisters to come up and go over the plans?" And one of the accountants, who was a bit of a problem, would ask me why this was necessary. I would say, "They are the ones who've got to make the plans work". On one occasion the charge sisters walked in, and here were all the plans laid out on the boardroom table. And I said to the architect, "Let's sit to one side and let them look at the plans". And he slid further and further down in his chair as the nurses pointed out things that were impractical. One said, "Oh, look where they have put the pan room; gosh, the kids will have to walk forever to get down there!"

'So we got their opinions, and it was better to find out the problems first, otherwise we would end up with costly building variations. The architect on this occasion made all the changes to his plans that were requested, and some of those wards are still the most economical places for the nurses to work. So we had the nurses' support – it wasn't a case of "us and them".'

Pixie had a great fondness for the 'kids' – the student nurses who were part of St Andrew's until 1986. The final graduation service at St Paul's Presbyterian Church took place in March 1986 for 27 graduating nurses, with the address by Pixie's old friend, Dr Pappy Walters. The School of Nursing was a considerable expense to the hospital, and with the Department of Nursing Studies by then well established at the Queensland Institute of Technology (later to become Queensland University of Technology) in Kelvin Grove, it was no longer necessary to train nurses at St Andrew's. Pixie supported the board's decision to close the school, with 525 graduates to its credit. This was also consistent with the long-running RANF campaign Pixie had helped wage to move nurse training to tertiary institutions. A few years after the school closed, Pixie and Bea Lemon organised a reunion of the St Andrew's Graduate Nurses' Association. The reunion took place in November 1989, and the guest of honour was St Andrew's first matron, Miss Dorothea Harrison. Much to the organisers' dismay, the get-together coincided with a pilot strike – but 350 graduates nevertheless were able to attend. It was the kind of occasion Pixie loved: a smart lunch and a day to recount stories from the wards and operating theatres of St Andrew's.

Pixie's last few years in charge at St Andrew's saw her absorb a huge amount of pressure as the hospital coped with the strains of high debt and changes to health funding by the Commonwealth government. There was never a time when money was not an issue, but with a board capably led by Bill Crawford and very able accountants, the hospital stayed afloat. The plan to build doctors' rooms across the road from the hospital in North Street went ahead. Property was purchased, and in 1988 the foundation stone for St Andrew's Place was unveiled by the Duke of Argyll, Ian Campbell. The Duke, chief of Clan Campbell and Scotland's second most senior duke, had been visiting Australia, and board chairman Dr Bill Crawford arranged for him to come to St Andrew's.

This continuation in connections to Queensland's Scottish community was a source of great pride for the hospital's supporters, in particular those who had been members of the Presbyterian Church. The amalgamation of the Congregational Union, Methodist and Presbyterian churches in Australia to form the Uniting Church had a big impact on St Andrew's. From 1977, the hospital's Board of Governors was drawn equally from the Uniting Church and a section of the Presbyterian Church that had chosen not to amalgamate. Then followed a legal dispute between the two churches over ownership of Emmanuel College at the University of Queensland. In spite of this tension, Presbyterian members continued to serve on the board of St Andrew's until 2000, when the Uniting Church came to a settlement with the Presbyterian Church and assumed full responsibility for the hospital.

Pixie, over all those years, had remained a faithful member of the Anglican Church in Lutwyche, and she observed the sadness this break caused: 'There were many people who were very upset and who couldn't understand what had happened. Some people stopped talking to each other. It was a painful period.' Having endured an acrimonious parting of ways with the RANF Queensland Branch Union of Employees (later known as the Queensland Nurses' Union), she understood how troubling 'break-ups' could be.

Most CEOs and senior executives survive for relatively short periods in the demanding field of health care. So Pixie's length of service was quite remarkable. In 1991, Pixie decided it was time to hand over the reins of St Andrew's: 'I said to the board one day, "I will make 1992 my last year". And they said, "You don't have to", but I felt it was the right thing to do.'

By the time Pixie retired from St Andrew's, the hospital was on a sound financial footing, thanks to the financial support of the Uniting Church and improvements in management of the hospital, which she and the board had put in place. Within a year of her departure, St Andrew's Place was completed and the sale of suites to doctors became a profitable venture.

Before leaving, Pixie managed the launch of numerous new facilities, including a cardiac rehabilitation unit, breast clinic, eye unit day ward, neurosurgical unit, MRI unit and a respite day care centre at Windsor. In her final year, 89 staff members received awards for employment of ten years or more, and this was a source of great pride for Pixie. By then she had completed several years' service as a surveyor of other hospitals for the Australian Council on Healthcare Standards: 'When I visited other hospitals around Australia, people used to be amazed when I told them that most of our charge sisters had worked for St Andrew's for ten to 15 years. One of my fellow surveyors who came to St Andrew's commented that in Victoria at that time, charge nurses usually remained in their jobs for about one year.'

It was with sadness but also relief that Pixie said goodbye as CEO of St Andrew's in July 1992. A huge celebratory lunch, attended by many of her friends and family, including Ellie, was held in the hospital's courtyard. Pixie felt quite exhausted from years and years of unrelenting hard work: 'There were 165 beds when I started. By the time I left, the hospital had doubled in size and we had 385 doctors who came to St Andrew's. One of the big changes during my time was improvement in surgery – as a result, patients had much shorter stays in hospital. There was also more appreciation for what nurses did for patients, but I had known this all along.'

## Chapter 9

# A Busy Retirement

## 1992–2014

When Pixie retired from St Andrew's in 1992, it was more a shift in gear than a true retirement. A few months after she left the hospital, Brisbane Archbishop Peter Hollingworth invited her to join the St Luke's Nursing Service Board – she went on to serve on the board for 13 years. It was the first of a number of positions she took up after her retirement. Visitors to her home in Everton Hills would observe that her dining room table was completely covered in documents and files – there were always more letters to write, jobs to complete, papers to file. She enjoyed being busy.

Her decision to join the board of St Luke's was motivated by her devotion to the Anglican Church and also her interest in care for the aged and in particular the work of community nurses who supported patients in their own homes. She had observed the work of community nurses from afar when patients were discharged from St Andrew's and recognised the important role they played in patient care. St Luke's had been part of Queensland's home nursing movement – caring for disadvantaged sick people, usually the elderly – for many years. At the time she joined the board, St Luke's Nursing Service had branches in the inner-Brisbane suburb of Milton as well as at Cleveland and Zillmere and employed about 40 people. Joining St Luke's board was a natural progression for Pixie, and her health management knowledge and personal contacts were of great use as St Luke's Nursing Service worked to expand its services and attract more funding.

In 1996, St Luke's appointed Cheryl Herbert as director of nursing and CEO. During her ten years at the helm, the organisation grew from a cottage industry organisation with a turnover of $3.5 million to a large provider of health and social services with an annual turnover of more than $100 million. Cheryl said she felt that Pixie 'took a gamble' appointing her in her first appointment at such a senior level. At that time Cheryl had a young family, including a three-year-old son, so 'really, the family also became part of St Luke's, and she always supported me'. Pixie's brief to the young leader was to 'make St Luke's viable and to grow it', because competitors were circling to buy out the organisation: 'Pixie was with me every step of the way. She taught me about the political environment, and I mean political with a small "p". She was my mentor, and through her I gained my first board appointment, with Anglicare Northern Territory. She has inspired so many people, particularly women, to have a go, and it's through her own example. She had amazing energy, she never stopped.'

The pair travelled extensively in the northern and western regions of Queensland to investigate opportunities for St Luke's to expand its services where gaps in delivery were evident. Cheryl recalled: 'We were at a motel way up north once, and when we were going to sleep, she asked me if I would mind putting a couch up against the door because she was a sleepwalker. I didn't quite believe this, but sure enough in the middle of the night, the couch rattled and she was trying to get out. She said, "I've been found on a main road and I didn't know I was there".'

Cheryl also recalled Pixie's love of a Scotch: 'We'd sit and have a whisky together and talk … And while she was our board chair, she also got involved supporting homeless women through the Lady Musgrave Trust.'

After a few years' service on St Luke's board, Pixie suggested the creation of an ethics committee for the nursing service, believing that clear ethical standards should guide decision-making, including choices about research projects. In 1996, she became the first chair of the St Luke's Ethics Committee, which was later to be known as the Anglicare Ethics Committee.

'During my work on the board of St Luke's, which became part of Spiritus-Anglicare and later Anglicare Southern Queensland, we had to approve research projects, and we needed ethical principles on which to base our decisions. Of course, I approached many people I knew well – doctors, nurses, leaders in the Church, lawyers and even philosophers – to help us as we developed the ethical principles for research projects where St Luke's, and later Anglicare, were involved. I had always been very interested in ethical standards, and at St Andrew's Dr Ken Jamieson and I had set up an ethics committee.'

Pixie took responsibility for formulating an ethical charter for St Luke's and steered it towards operating under the guidelines of the National Health and Medical Research Council. For 15 years, she attended monthly meetings to consider research projects submitted by university and hospital researchers to St Luke's and later Anglicare. By 2010, Anglicare had become a significant organisation with a workforce of about 2,000 people, employed in residential aged care, community care and other social services. During her time with Anglicare's Human Research Ethics Committee, she supported many new initiatives, including care for older people in rural communities, support for people with HIV/AIDS and homelessness programs.

'With the ethics committee, we had to think carefully about what effect the research would have on our clients. That was always our first priority. For example, over the years we have received many requests to do dementia studies because we have dementia patients in our various villages. Sometimes we had to say no because it takes staff time and, apart from that, we didn't want people to become exhausted and stressed by being questioned all the time.'

Pixie, an early supporter of IVF, continued her interest in human research ethical principles. In 1999, the Queensland Fertility Group appointed her chair of its Human Research and Ethics Committee, a position she occupied for ten years: 'I knew Dr John Hennessy very well, and we already had an ethics committee established at St Andrew's that managed IVF, so I was very interested when Queensland Fertility Group asked me to sit on this new committee.'

Pixie's ability to attract bright minds to serve on committees was part of her well-honed skill in managing people. Jennifer West, a nurse and friend from her days at St Andrew's and from the Zonta Club of Brisbane South (which is committed to advancing the status of women) to which they both belonged, commented that 'you never want to see Pixie walking towards you or you'll end up on a committee'.

'She was a little pocket dynamo. She got me involved with the Queensland Fertility Group Human Research and Ethics Committee because I was a researcher – at that stage I was an Industry Fellow at the University of Queensland and running the cardiovascular genetic clinic at Prince Charles Hospital. So she thought that I would be a good person to have on the committee. Then she recruited me onto the Anglicare Southern Queensland Human Research Ethics Committee, which she still chairs. She was very much instrumental in putting those two ethics committees for large organisations on the map.'

Jennifer often observed Pixie in action: 'She does not shy away from men or doctors or anyone really. She was able to just take on board what they had to say, and if they were stroppy she was able to handle that in a way that wasn't offensive – that's really been one of her very strong points. As far as recruitment of ethics personnel, she was not backward in coming forward in approaching philosophers, lawyers, church people, you name it, to come onto the committees. And it was thanks to Pixie that St Luke's became the first community nursing agency to provide in-home care for people with HIV/AIDS in Queensland after winning a state government tender.'

Pixie loved her work with St Luke's and Anglicare: 'I was always passionate about care of the aged. These people have lived in a less prosperous Australia, working at their first job for less than a few dollars a week. They fought world wars and the Great Depression and paid for their own homes without government assistance. Today they are looked on as a burden to the taxpayer. I find that insulting. They are the ones responsible for helping establish our wealthy country. They are entitled to comfort and the best care possible, and I will continue to advocate for them.'

Over the years, Pixie had developed a great love of the St Andrew's Nursing Home – and its closure in 1998 was a sad day for her. When it closed its doors, Pixie attended a farewell lunch at the home she had come to know so well and where her parents had both died. She accepted these changes with her usual practical approach, recognising that 'all good things come to an end'.

In 2001, Pixie squeezed in time to get involved with yet another organisation, Older People Speak Out (OPSO), established by her friend, journalist and journalism teacher Val French.

Val first got to know Pixie well in the mid-1980s when they started working together to campaign for better treatment for nursing home residents, and Pixie involved Val on a committee established by St Luke's to assess standards of nursing home care. Pixie regarded Val French as inspirational, and a good friend: 'I had the greatest respect for her. Val fought for years to highlight the marginalisation of older people. She was a journalist and founder of the School of Journalism at Queensland University of Technology, and was always very good at collaborating on projects, so if you went anywhere with her, to any town, she had contacts in the media, with seniors groups, and so on.

'In the early 2000s, Val and I were on an OPSO committee looking at housing for people in the regions, and during this time we had a lot of meetings with the Queensland government, including with a very elegant gentleman in the Department of Housing. We were proposing the development of public housing in regional towns so that older people could remain where they have been all their adult lives, rather than come to the city to get a roof over their heads. We had a discussion that went round and round with this man, it was a very frustrating process, and in the end we did not get it off the ground.'

Pixie was also involved in highlighting the problems experienced by the elderly trying to eat their meals in public hospitals in Queensland: 'It never occurs to people how difficult it is for frail patients to open lids, pick up cups and manage their food. So for two years, three of us, Joy Wilson, Fran Ryan and I, went out as volunteers for a few hours once a week to The Prince Charles Hospital, a hospital I have great affection and respect for, and helped out in the extended care area. It wasn't practical to keep doing this indefinitely, because we all had so many other commitments, but we kept highlighting the issue in meetings with Queensland Health. As a result of our efforts, we attracted some publicity from Channel Ten about the problem generally, and improvements were made to arrangements in the extended care area.'

In 2005, Pixie was appointed to the Anglicare Community Services Commission, which oversees aged care in Anglicare homes throughout the Brisbane Diocese, the community nursing service and the welfare services: 'We meet every month and I report to them on the work of the ethics committee and my role on occasion on the Anglicare Care Governance Committee.'

In all these and a multitude of other commitments, Pixie was driven by a desire to be involved, to make a difference, to make sure people don't forget. And so, for many years she and a small group of ex-nurse colleagues have maintained the Museum of Nursing History, housed until 2014 in the old Lady Lamington Nurses' Home at the Royal Brisbane Hospital. Cecelia Brazil, who was the former acting director of nursing of the RBH, was the first curator of the nursing museum and worked tirelessly to amass the collection. Pixie became Honorary Secretary of the RBH Nurses' Association in 1998: 'We felt it was important to preserve the history because we lived through it. I firmly believe that an understanding of history has a big effect on attitudes and occurrences.'

On 20 October 2014, Australian Governor-General Sir Peter Cosgrove opened an exhibition featuring ex-World War I staff from the RBH, and he visited the museum, which had been relocated from the Lady Lamington Nurses'

Home to the former Ward 7 at the RBH. Before the relocation, a small band of RBH Nurses' Association Committee members and other volunteers, including Pixie, worked for weeks to pack up the extensive collection and move it to the new museum: 'It was an exhausting job. We were very sad to move – the Lady Lamington Nurses' Home had been a very historic site for so long. We had all lived there. There were so many memories up there. It was the end of an era.'

Another building in Brisbane with a history Pixie appreciated was the Lady Musgrave Lodge at 35 Astor Terrace in Spring Hill. For almost 100 years, the Lady Musgrave Lodge was a home for young women – in its early years it was a refuge for migrants arriving by boat, and it later became a home for women from country areas who came to work and study in Brisbane.

Pixie knew the attractive, two-storey, Nicholson and Wright-designed building well – it was close to many doctors' rooms on Wickham Terrace and a short stroll down the hill from St Andrew's. She also knew a young woman who had lived in the home.

'I knew a seamstress from Woombye who lived at the Lady Musgrave Lodge; my parents were friends of her parents, so my parents drove her to the lodge when she first took up residence there in the late 1940s.'

The Lady Musgrave Lodge Committee was first established in 1885 under the patronage of Lady Lucinda Musgrave, wife of the Queensland Governor, to provide accommodation for mainly migrant women, and the Lady Musgrave Home in Spring Hill opened in 1892 to 'provide a home for friendless girls'.

By 1975, Lady Musgrave Lodge was gone from Spring Hill during an era when historic buildings were often demolished in Brisbane. The demolition came three years after the Lady Musgrave Lodge Committee had decided to close the home because of declining resident numbers, building deterioration and mounting financial losses. However, the demise of this historic home was not the end of Lady Musgrave's vision.

The Lady Musgrave Trust was formed in 1997 to manage the funds received from the proceeds of the sale, with the vision of continuing to provide accommodation for homeless young women. One of the board trustees was Pixie's good friend, auctioneer and real estate agent John Meldrum, who had managed the sale of the lodge. He had often helped St Andrew's acquire property around Spring Hill, and Pixie knew him well.

'I didn't even know the Lady Musgrave Trust existed. John Meldrum, who was the president of the Trust, rang and asked if I would consider serving on the board – at that stage I had more than enough to keep me busy. But John had been a good friend to St Andrew's, so I agreed to come on the board.'

As usual with any project Pixie took on, she not only joined the board, she embraced the vision of the Trust and increased her awareness of the problems associated with homelessness.

The Lady Musgrave Trust wanted to focus on bricks and mortar projects rather than entering into the realm of service provision, and they had tried unsuccessfully to develop partnerships with organisations working with homeless people. Pixie, who was by then well-established on the board of St Luke's Nursing Service, suggested they approach St Luke's Anglicare. Bernard Yorke, who was manager of the Brisbane Diocese, met with the Lady Musgrave Trust Board in 1998. Shortly after this, Pixie negotiated an agreement with Anglicare whereby the Trust would purchase the buildings to accommodate homeless people and Anglicare would provide the support service. It became a very successful arrangement that provided housing for young women who were homeless or at risk of homelessness in Brisbane.

Pixie was not only good at the business of creating partnerships, she enjoyed identifying suitable buildings and building projects. The Trust purchased a block of six townhouses in Nundah in August 1998 to provide homes for young women, aged 14 to 25, including any of their children, in need.

'One Friday, I set off with one of the social workers from Anglicare. I said, "We'll spend from 8.00 am to 1.00 pm, and if we haven't found anything by then, we'll go home". So we hunted high and low. We wanted a place that was preferably empty, and it wasn't easy to find an empty block of units. As we were driving through Nundah, we stopped at a real estate agent and I went in and said, "I'd like a unit block with at least six units, but they must have their own little gardens because I want the girls to be independent". He looked at me and said, "You don't want much, do you?" He said it was impossible. I said, "Well, see what you can do". As we drove along about a mile further on, I saw this building near the park. I went over and it had a "for sale" sign on it, it was brand-new, it was six townhouses. So I found out who the owner was and that it had been spec built. I rang John Meldrum – he came out and thought it looked like a good buy, and we still have them.'

Bishop John Noble conducted the official opening of the home in May 1999: 'One of the residents there was a young woman with a little boy of about three. I asked her their names and she introduced me to Luke. She said to me, "You have no idea what it's like to walk up those stairs and feel safe. For the last two years, I've been in a flat where I couldn't lock the door properly and the windows didn't shut. That was all I could afford. Luke was getting to the stage where he wouldn't sleep because he was terrified someone would come through the door. You have no idea what a comfort this place is".'

There was still money in the Trust for another project, so in September 2001 Pixie received a call from her friend John Meldrum: 'He asked me to look at a property near Kalinga that the Trust wanted to buy. So I agreed to meet him to inspect the units, but he never arrived for our appointment. He had died that morning, just collapsed and died. Of course, I was devastated because he had been my friend for years. Then I got talked into taking over as president, to follow John. I thought, "There is no use doing things by halves, you've got to be in it", and so I agreed and I was lucky to work with a very hard-working committee.'

And so, at the age of 71, Pixie became president of the Lady Musgrave Trust, a position she held for the next 13 years: 'We ended up not buying the building John had in mind – I had to go searching for another one because the one he was thinking of buying was strata titled and it still had eight people in it. I had mental visions of trying to do deals with eight people and trying to get them out of the place. We finally bought a block of six two-bedroom units in 2003 in Windsor, and we named it in honour of John Meldrum.'

Over the years, the Lady Musgrave Trust identified a need for more collaboration with like-minded organisations, and in 2006 it signed an agreement with the Sisters of the Good Samaritan to work together to support homeless young women. In 2009, the Lady Musgrave Trust hosted and chaired the first Homeless Forum, and these have become annual events designed to better co-ordinate the many organisations that work in this sector. Trustee Judy Magub, a former Brisbane City Councillor, was instrumental in convening several of the forums. Pixie explained: 'We wanted to create a network where we could support each other and connect, and it became clear that many people were frustrated trying to meet the needs of women, especially those in crisis and short-term accommodation. Judy Magub really led the project to improve co-ordination.

'One of the Lady Musgrave Trust's other great supporters is Joy Chambers Grundy, who as champion of the Trust is supportive and generous. She and her husband, Reg Grundy, live in Bermuda, and when she visits Australia every year she always makes an effort to attend our events.'

# MAKING YOU FEEL AT HOME

**One of the special contributions of the St. Andrew's Auxiliary is a little extra touch of comfort for patients and their families in the streamlined and efficient modern Hospital.**

The Kiosk in the courtyard has been in operation for over a year now, providing somewhere pleasant and restful for visitors, Hospital staff, and walking patients to relax with a cup of tea or coffee and a snack. (The snack is often something home-made, to a good old Scottish or Australian traditional recipe).

For many country visitors, who may have driven long distances without stopping for meals, the Kiosk provides an important service.

The new "Amber Room", on the other side of the courtyard, near Wickham Terrace, will extend this service.

### COMFORT

In many other ways the Auxiliary continues to provide important services for the Hospital.

Many patients are probably not aware that the curtains at their window, the gowns worn by patients (and surgeons and nursing staff) in the theatres, and most of the Hospital soft furnishings have been made by the ladies of the Hospital Sewing Bees.

This contribution of skill and devoted service has added greatly to the comfort and appearance of the Hospital, and saves thousands of dollars a year.

And the hard-working nursing staff, as well as patients, have many reasons to be grateful for the visitors on the Flower roster, who look after the flowers given to patients.

## COURTYARD KIOSK

*The Courtyard Kiosk at St. Andrew's is an excellent place to relax, and not too far for walking patients to come to entertain visiting members of their families. Friendly service and good cooking are provided by members of St. Andrew's Auxiliary.*

The St Andrew's Auxiliary and the Kiosk, where Ellie often worked, featured in the *St Andrew's Messenger* in December 1979.

# SO WELL REMEMBERED

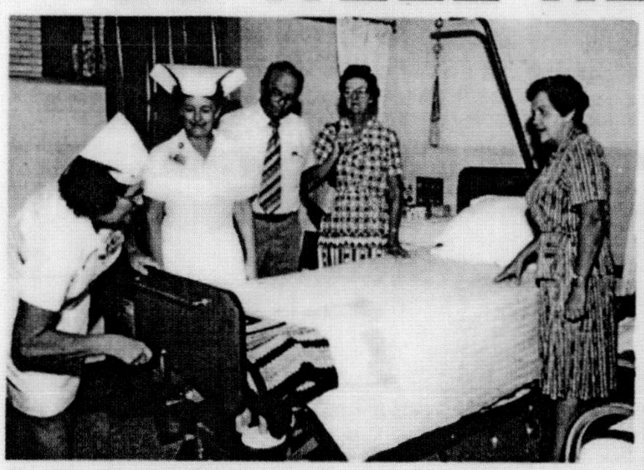

*The late Mr. and Mrs. James Whamond Annat had a long and sympathetic interest in the work of St. Andrew's War Memorial Hospital, and at the end of their lives were patients in St. Andrew's Nursing Home. Family and friends remembered this when it came to selecting a tribute to their memory, and in both cases selected a gift that will be of great use to future patients. (At left) Mrs. Annat's three children see a demonstration of the special adjustable bed they gave in memory of their mother from donations in her memory. Sister Ruth Nugent and Sister Lilian McNaughton demonstrate, watched by Mr. Don Annat, Mrs. Ellen Murr, and Miss Isobel Annat. (Right) Mrs. Deborah Ann Crozier enjoys a book selected from the handsome bookcase given to St. Andrew's Nursing Home by Mr. Annat's friends. Mrs. Crozier was for 25 years a member of St. Andrew's Sewing groups.*

In August 1981, the *St Andrew's Messenger* paid tribute to Pixie's parents, who had both passed away at St Andrew's Nursing Home. They had had a long association with the hospital. The photograph on the left features Pixie, Ellie and Don.

Pixie examining paintings for a forthcoming St Andrew's art show, mid-1980s. The art shows were held at St Andrew's every year.

St Andrew's held its 21st student nurse graduation ceremony in March 1980 in the hospital garden area.

ANZAC Day service at St Andrew's War Memorial Hospital, April 1980.
Pixie's mother, Madoline Annat, is seated in a wheelchair in the front row.

Pixie (in pink dress) with a student nurse group, 1981.

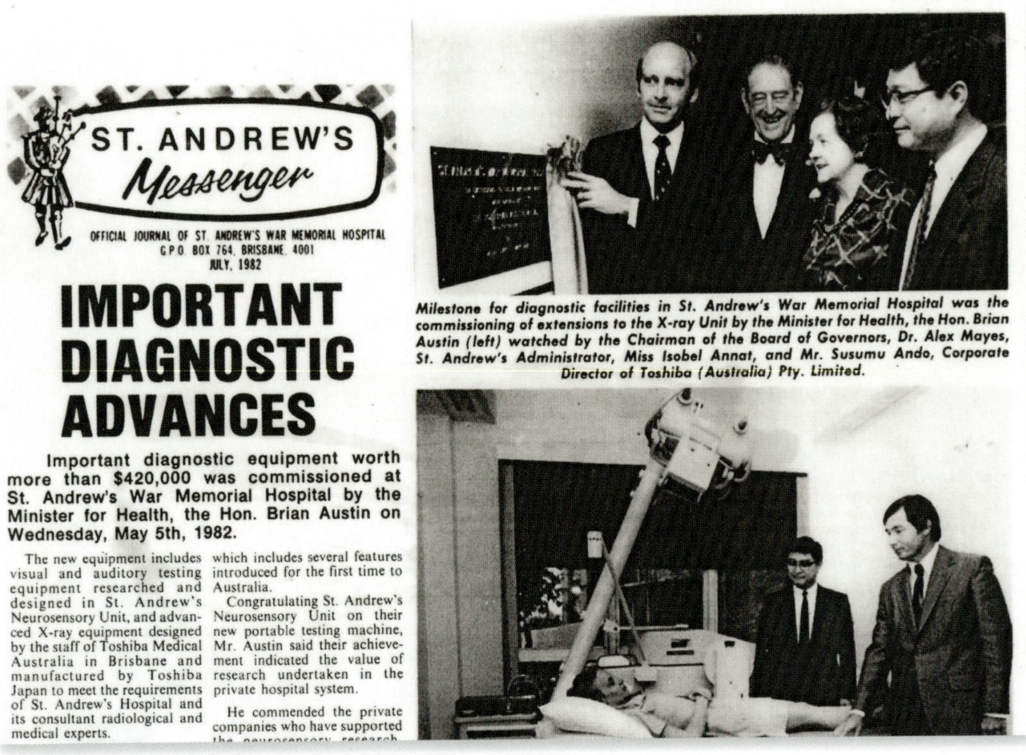

ST. ANDREW'S
*Messenger*

OFFICIAL JOURNAL OF ST. ANDREW'S WAR MEMORIAL HOSPITAL
G.P.O. BOX 764, BRISBANE, 4001
JULY, 1982

# IMPORTANT DIAGNOSTIC ADVANCES

**Important diagnostic equipment worth more than $420,000 was commissioned at St. Andrew's War Memorial Hospital by the Minister for Health, the Hon. Brian Austin on Wednesday, May 5th, 1982.**

The new equipment includes visual and auditory testing equipment researched and designed in St. Andrew's Neurosensory Unit, and advanced X-ray equipment designed by the staff of Toshiba Medical Australia in Brisbane and manufactured by Toshiba Japan to meet the requirements of St. Andrew's Hospital and its consultant radiological and medical experts.

which includes several features introduced for the first time to Australia.

Congratulating St. Andrew's Neurosensory Unit on their new portable testing machine, Mr. Austin said their achievement indicated the value of research undertaken in the private hospital system.

He commended the private companies who have supported

***Milestone for diagnostic facilities in St. Andrew's War Memorial Hospital was the commissioning of extensions to the X-ray Unit by the Minister for Health, the Hon. Brian Austin (left) watched by the Chairman of the Board of Governors, Dr. Alex Mayes, St. Andrew's Administrator, Miss Isobel Annat, and Mr. Susumu Ando, Corporate Director of Toshiba (Australia) Pty. Limited.***

During her time at the helm of St Andrew's, Pixie worked to ensure the hospital had the latest medical equipment and expertise. In 1982, the *St Andrew's Messenger* announced the commissioning of new diagnostic facilities for St Andrew's.

Dr Harold Crawford (right), the first chairman of St Andrew's, photographed in the 1950s. His son, Dr Bill Crawford (far right), succeeded Dr Alex Mayes in the 1980s.

Left to right: Dr Leigh Atkinson, Dr Bill Crawford, Elwin Crawford, Lady Joy Killen, Sir James Killen, Pixie and Ron Glenney at the 1987 annual St Andrew's dinner.

Pixie in her office at St Andrew's on the day of her retirement in July 1992.

The St Andrew's Auxiliary ladies and gentleman
farewell the hospital's much-admired leader.

This cartoon featured in a farewell article on Pixie published in the *St Andrew's Messenger* in 1992.

In 1994, Pixie travelled to Gallipoli to remember her father and uncles who had served in World War I.

Pixie (back row, second from the left), Lady Musgrave Trust Board President, with fellow board members, 2000.

ABOVE: In August 2001, Pixie travelled to Elands River, South Africa, to unveil plaques honouring her grandfather's bravery in the second Anglo-Boer war.

LEFT: The memorial for Lieutenant James Whamond Annat, Pixie's grandfather, August 2001.

BELOW: Photographed at the 2001 Kedron Wavell RBH dinner for returned nurses are (left to right) Mark and Libby Odling, Ron Glenney, Pixie Annat and Beth Dawson.

Left to right: St Andrew's Volunteer Manager Cathy Cash, Pixie, St Andrew's Auxiliary member and long-serving volunteer Win Westacott, then St Andrew's general manager Ian England and CEO of UnitingCare Queensland Anne Cross enjoying the 2008 Christmas function for St Andrew's Auxiliary members.

LEFT: Pixie speaking at the 2010 AGM of the Royal Brisbane Hospital Nurses' Association, held at the hospital's Education Centre.

BELOW: Friends helped Pixie celebrate her 80th birthday on 18 March 2010.

**RIGHT:** Representing the Nurses' Fund, Pixie casts a wreath at the *Centaur* At-Sea Service of Remembrance and Thanksgiving aboard HMAS *Manoora*, 24 September 2010.

**ABOVE AND RIGHT:** At the service, Pixie joined around 300 relatives of those who had served on the hospital ship that was torpedoed by a Japanese submarine on 14 May 1943 off Stradbroke Island.

LEFT: In 2012, a dinner was held to celebrate the 60th anniversary of Pixie's graduation from the Royal Brisbane Hospital.

BELOW: Annual service at St Andrew's Anglican Church, Lutwyche, for The Most Excellent Order of the British Empire Queensland Association, 2012. Pixie received an MBE in 1977 and a Medal of the Order of Australia (OAM) in 1992 for services to nursing.

Pixie as president of the Lady Musgrave Trust, 2013.

ABOVE: Pixie at the 2013 ANZAC Day service at St Andrew's.

RIGHT: Colleen Ryan Clur with Pixie at the 2014 St Andrew's ANZAC Day service.

Left to right: Pixie, Dr Humphrey Cramond and Prof. Tess Cramond at the biennial Bancroft Oration given by Prof. David Paterson in Brisbane, 27 November 2013.

Pixie at the 2013 Queensland Poppy Appeal, which highlighted the work of military nurses both past and present.

In March 2014, Ellie and Pixie celebrated their 84th birthday at the OBE Luncheon, Alexandra Headland Surf Lifesaving Club, Queensland.

On 18 November 2014, Pixie and fellow St Andrew's volunteer Darcy Howe received UnitingCare Queensland Moderator's Medals for outstanding community service. The ceremony was attended by many friends of St Andrew's, including Ellie (to Pixie's left) and Ellie's granddaughter, who is Pixie's great-niece, Jessica Murr (to her right).

Sharing the special day with Ellie.

In 2014, Pixie relinquished her role as president of the Lady Musgrave Trust and became Vice-President, Community Relations. Fellow board member Bernard Yorke, who was 'roped in' to serve on the Trust by Pixie, said: 'She is very astute, she has a great understanding of human propensities and other people's thinking. On the Trust you get different views, and she consulted widely. She's been involved with caring for people all her life, I think. She cares for nurses who care for people, too. She's been a great asset to Queensland.'

Volumes could be written on any of Pixie's diverse activities as a volunteer. However, if she were to pick out her key interest, the Committee of the Centaur Memorial Fund for Nurses would be near the top of the list. Her interest in the Centaur work brought together several strands of her life: nursing, military service, education and remembrance.

She and Ellie had been proud fundraisers as part of the Centaur Younger Set in the 1940s and 1950s, and their parents were active Centaur Memorial Fund Committee members for many years. The purchase and opening of Centaur House in Queen Street, Brisbane, in 1947 created a professional centre for nurses, of which Pixie had been a part. She had worked at Centaur House as secretary of the RANF in the early 1960s and attended countless meetings on nursing matters in this building with her RANF colleagues. In 1971, the original building was sold and a new Centaur House in Wickham Terrace was built; it served as a centre for nurses until 1979.

Pixie, who had joined the Centaur Committee in 1975, supported the decision to sell the building and invest the funds to provide scholarships for nurses: 'I was invited to join the Centaur Memorial Fund Committee, and later we decided to make it a living memorial by offering an annual $15,000 scholarship so that nurses could undertake postgraduate study. We felt this was in keeping with the memory of all those, but particularly the 11 nurses, who had died on the *Centaur*. It has been a continuation, to make sure Centaur remains a living memorial.'

Pixie helped guide the investment of moneys to ensure the scholarship fund was financially sound. Her interest in promoting postgraduate study was shaped by her many years of fighting for better nurse education, and she was influenced by the contacts she had made with nurse academics from abroad. Coming from a generation that had not had the luxury of university study, she was determined to promote nursing as a recognised field of study. From 2003 until 2008, the patron of the Centaur Committee was the Governor of Queensland, Quentin Bryce, and she attended annual meetings where the Fellowship Award was presented.

'Dame Quentin Bryce always took a big interest in nursing and medical matters. As a young woman she had taken part in St Andrew's doorknock appeals, and our paths often crossed over the years. It meant a lot to us that she came to Centaur annual meetings – I think she appreciated that we provided scholarship support for nurses, many of whom went on to have significant academic careers. Queensland Governor Penelope Wensley, as the next patron, also attended Centaur commemorative services in Brisbane and Townsville.

The first Centaur Fellowship recipient (in 1993) was Elizabeth Beattie, who went on to become a Professor of Nursing at Queensland University of Technology. She undertook her masters and PhD with the help of a Centaur Fellowship and enjoyed a distinguished academic career in the United States before returning to Australia.

'Elizabeth is internationally recognised, and she has taught a generation of Queensland students many aspects of clinical nursing. She also took a big interest in ethics and aged care, and her work with people suffering from dementia is well recognised. The Centaur Committee is proud of the role we had in supporting nurses and academics like Elizabeth, and of course she remains a member of the Centaur Committee.'

Professor Linda Shields, now a Professor of Nursing (Tropical Health) at James Cook University, was another early recipient of a Centaur Fellowship. Her work has focused on care of children in health services and on the history of nursing. She has won many awards, including a Churchill Fellowship, but believes the Centaur Fellowship helped launch her academic career. Like Elizabeth Beattie, Linda later joined the Centaur Committee.

Linda acknowledged the value of the Centaur Fellowship: 'Every nurse in Brisbane knew Pixie because of who she was, but of course we would never have dreamed of calling her Pixie, she was always Miss Annat. In 1996, I won a Centaur Fellowship and that's when I really got to know Pixie. Centaur helped get my PhD completed, and the only thing the committee wanted back from us was to support them and turn up at the commemorative services if we could. I have done this as best as I could – I have travelled back from England to attend a service. Pixie was really the mover and shaker in getting the fellowships going. She contributed significantly to the development of nursing education in

Australia. She had a real awareness of the need for tertiary education for nurses, and for nurses to get PhDs so nursing could become a really credible profession. I think that is what drove her to get all this going. She made it all happen; not her alone, but she was one of the ones who made it all happen in Queensland – she has made a huge contribution to nursing.'

Another recipient who later became a member of the Centaur Committee was Griffith University Associate Professor Marion Mitchell. According to Marion: 'The Centaur Fellowship is still regarded as one of the best scholarships to get in the field of nursing. $15,000 is a considerable sum of money and there are no strings attached, within reason.'

Marion joined the committee the year she was awarded the fellowship, 2003. 'Sometimes when I'm driving home from a two-hour Centaur meeting, I think to myself that we could have got through the business a lot faster – they tend to go off on tangents – but then I think how much of a privilege it is to be around these women, and Pixie in particular. They have these little anecdotes to share and it's just so interesting. It's wonderful to be around them.'

Another sacred aspect of Centaur is the annual commemorative service, usually held at the St Andrew's Anglican Church at Lutwyche where Pixie worships. For major anniversaries, such as the 60th and 70th anniversaries of the sinking of the AHS *Centaur*, commemorative services were held in St John's Cathedral in Brisbane. There were always stories exchanged at these treasured gatherings, going back to the family members who were lost with the sinking of the *Centaur* on 14 May 1943. At the 60th anniversary service, Pixie spoke to a woman whose mother's first husband, a doctor, had died on the *Centaur*.

'By this stage, the woman was in a wheelchair. She told me she had never come to a commemorative service before then because it upset her too much. She said to me that day, "It occurred to me that if 1,000 people could think it important enough to come to the Cathedral today, the least I could do was turn up". She died shortly after this service. There were always these personal stories.'

Pixie also took an interest in the Centaur Naval Cadets based in Maleny in the Sunshine Coast Hinterland, not far from where she had grown up in Palmwoods: 'We started making a presentation shield available for the cadet with the greatest potential. They've developed a very smart naval unit up there, and they train at Mooloolaba. Most of the cadets are still at high school, but they really get a kick out of this activity. They parade every year in December at the showgrounds in Maleny, and a Centaur Memorial Fund Committee member presents the award to the most promising cadet.'

For years, Pixie followed the efforts made in trying to locate the wreck of the *Centaur*. In 2009, with the help of $4 million from the federal and Queensland governments, the wreck was finally located by a team headed by David Mearns. The wreck was found 30 nautical miles east of the southern tip of Moreton Island, at least 1,800 metres down.

'At the time they found the *Centaur* I was on holiday in my time-share unit up at Caloundra, and I received a call from Channel 7 to say that the wreck had been located. After all these years of many false sightings, this was amazing news. I could hardly believe it.'

On 12 January 2010, David Mearns's team laid a memorial plaque on the foredeck of the *Centaur*, which had rested undisturbed for 66 years. Incorporated in the plaque was a roll of honour with the names of the 268 people who had died. There was also extensive filming of the wreck, and on this last day of filming, divers found personal items: ankle boots with the laces intact, a trunk of personal belongings and a felt slouch hat. The discovery of these items touched everybody involved in the search – it reminded them of the humanity of those who had died so long ago. David Mearns said at the time that 'one of the great privileges in my life was to have led this important project'.

The service at sea was followed by a national memorial service held at St John's Cathedral in March 2010 attended by 600 people. Those there to pay their respects included members of the Centaur Committee and serving dignitaries, including then Australian Governor-General Quentin Bryce, Queensland Governor Penelope Wensley and then Prime Minister Kevin Rudd. In September 2010, Pixie attended a special ceremony for relatives that was held aboard HMAS *Manoora*. Wreaths were laid and the ashes of three survivors scattered during the service, close to the resting place of the *Centaur*.

'It was an incredible experience, the ship went out and it was motionless over the site of the *Centaur*. A young woman came up to me and asked me what I was thinking about. I told her I was thinking about the girls down there and how useless it was that the ship was sunk. There were hundreds of people on board, remembering relatives, who had every reason to be very sad. One woman came up to me and said, "So what do you do with your committee?" She told me she was from Adelaide and that her father had died on the *Centaur*. And while she was speaking to me there was a woman sitting about two rows back, listening to our conversation. The woman who was seated had travelled to the service from Perth. She said, "Excuse me, did you say your name was 'so and so'?" They realised they were cousins. Their fathers had both served in the war and their families had not kept in touch. It was the sort of thing that happened that day, it was rather special.'

One of Pixie's good friends, Fran Ryan, who was '2-I.C.' to Pixie in the Royal Brisbane Hospital's private wards in the early 1960s, recalled how much the service at sea meant to her friend: 'The day Pixie went out on the boat to lay the wreath for the *Centaur* was one of the highlights of her life. She came home that night and rang me straight away. She was just so pleased, it meant so much to her.'

## Conclusion

# Still Living Life to the Full

In 2002, Pixie sold her house in Everton Hills and bought an eighth-floor unit in Kelvin Grove, in a 1970s-style building. Her modest but comfortable home is filled with photographs, documents, books and, of course, her Royal Doulton china. At night, she loves to see the twinkling lights from the suburbs of Brisbane where she lived for most of her life.

Pixie's unit is halfway between the Royal Brisbane Hospital (RBH) and St Andrew's War Memorial Hospital – the two places where she has given and received so much. Her home suits her perfectly, and well into her 80s she continues to bustle about, serving on committees, meeting friends at bridge and bowls, volunteering, living her life to the full. She continues to return regularly to the RBH, for meetings of the RBH Nurses' Association and to volunteer in the Museum of Nursing History.

In 2007, she began serving as an early-morning volunteer at St Andrew's. At 5.45 am every Thursday, Pixie drives to St Andrew's for her two-hour volunteer shift that commences at 6.00 am. She helps ease new patients into the rhythm of St Andrew's as she escorts them through the twists and turns of the hospital, delivering them to wards and departments that she knows better than anyone else.

'Volunteering at St Andrew's is interesting, and people often ask me about the history of the hospital. One woman said to me the other day, "You look like an old nurse". I wasn't sure how to take that.'

It was thanks to Pixie that St Andrew's launched its patient escort service 30 years ago: 'We realised that patients needed help when they arrive – not just

St Andrew's, but many other hospitals began providing this service in the 1980s. People get very lost in hospitals, because many of them were built in stages and they can be hard to navigate. Also, patients when they are being admitted are thinking of something else, the reason they are coming to hospital, and so if you are there to help, then patients don't have to worry about where to go.'

Looking back at nursing, Pixie believes that the profession has not really changed, and nor has her philosophy: 'It's about the care you give to the patient as an individual. That hasn't changed. The training has changed – earlier it was by the hospital method, now it is through academic study and some practical experience – I believe this practical experience needs to be extended.

'I have always told nurses that the patient must feel that the person caring for them knows them, knows what they are doing and does it with a smile. I used to say to the student nurses, "Never talk to another person over a patient in bed, even if you think they are unconscious". Often they can hear what you are saying even if they can't convey it to you.'

Pixie has always committed completely to everything she takes on. This includes her membership of the OBE Queensland Association, which she joined after receiving a Member of the Most Excellent Order of the British Empire in 1977 and Medal of the Order of Australia in 1992 for services to nursing. As president of the OBE Queensland Association since 2002, she arranged regular lunches for members. She is a great host, and anyone who attends a lunch is familiar with the 'Pixie touch'. Visitors to her unit are offered hot, strong tea served in her bone china cups, and there is always a treat: a slice of cake or one of her curried egg sandwiches, served on a well-pressed tablecloth.

Pixie has been a devoted member of St Andrew's Anglican Church in Lutwyche her entire adult life, serving as a member of Synod and a Parish councillor, and she continues to volunteer at the church. Reverend Sandra Kjellgren, rector of the parish since 2001, views Pixie as a mentor and friend:

'She is a woman of capacity, intelligence and amazing leadership ability, yet she is so humble; she will come to the church and give two hours' administrative help in the office or help with anything else that needs doing. That is the spirituality of Pixie. She has been the most brilliant Parish councillor who doesn't know the word defeat. Even if something looks insurmountable, Pixie's attitude is "give it a go". I lost my parents and other close family members within a three-year period. At the same time we were dealing with the Northern Busway Airport Link Project on the doorstep of the church. We were surrounded by construction on three sides – they were tunnelling and blasting – the dust and noise were horrendous. I was struggling to grieve and to do anything. And Pixie personally gave me the most amazing support by sharing how she dealt with the demise of her parents. I am a priest, and she ministered to me in a way I would minister to others. It came out of her deep spirituality and her nursing background … You can't know Pixie and not love her, I don't think.'

The stories Pixie can tell about her life are almost endless, because she has an excellent memory for names and a flare for funny or moving details. Two important stories in her later life were overseas trips to remember her grandfather, and father and uncles, who served in the world wars.

In 1994, she used the money that was collected as a farewell gift by St Andrew's doctors to pay for her trip to Gallipoli. Alone, she flew to London and then to Istanbul: 'The next day I travelled to Gallipoli, and I was the only person on the bus – the guide and the driver were both marvellous to me. I was surprised at how similar the scenery was – it could have been anywhere in Queensland.

'It gave me the most extraordinary feeling of going back in time when I went to Gallipoli and read the words written to the mothers of the world by Kemal Atatürk, who was the President of Turkey and Colonel at Gallipoli, on the Commonwealth Military Graves Memorial. He said: *"Your sons are now lying in our bosom and are at peace. After having lost their lives on this land, they have become our sons as well."* That was very moving. I visited Lone Pine, which Dad had often spoken about. I tried to imagine how they survived it at all, with those conditions, when all they had to eat was bully beef and biscuits.'

In August 2001, 101 years after her grandfather, James Whamond Annat, had died in the second Anglo-Boer war, Pixie travelled to South Africa as a guest of a local South African history group, to attend the unveiling of two plaques erected in honour of James.

She landed in Johannesburg on a sunny winter's day. Once again she was struck by the landscape, which was not dissimilar to Queensland – there were jacaranda trees in bloom and gum trees, both foreign species, now firmly planted in African soil.

Pixie travelled with her hosts to Elands River, through dry, rugged terrain, for the unveiling of the memorial plaques on the very place where her grandfather had died defending the British supply depot so long ago: 'I was given the honour of unveiling the plaques and afterwards I was asked, "What are you thinking about?" I replied, "It was a very harsh place in which to die". The Boer general and future Prime Minister Jan Smuts once said about the siege at Elands River that "never in the course of the Boer war did a besieged force endure worse suffering, and yet stood their ground with magnificent courage".

'I said to the chaplain conducting the service for Grandfather's plaque, "Why would you do this? He was the enemy". He replied, "Because he was so brave".

'I was just touched by the warm welcome given to me by all the South Africans, those who were part of this local history group and others I met on my trip. I came home wondering whether Australians would have made similar arrangements as the South Africans did, for a former enemy.'

Looking back on her life, Pixie has few regrets. She derived happiness from every friendship, and in particular her relationship with Ellie. For years they have kept up the habit of phoning each other – once in the morning and once in the afternoon, just to talk – and they have participated in countless activities together.

Many of Pixie's close friends and family have died in recent years, including her brother, Donald, and her brother-in-law, Bruce Murr. Pixie has felt these losses deeply. But she remains positive and in touch with many friends. She is also very close to and fond of Ellie's grandchildren, Jessica and Christine. Pixie and Ellie, now in their mid-80s, still often attend rowing regattas to watch these young women in competition.

Pixie never sought out recognition and believes everything she achieved has been a team effort. When asked what has motivated her, she replied: 'My parents were very interested in everything, and so was I. I've always been curious about things, and I've never had time to sit around and do nothing.'

# Credits

## IMAGES

Lieutenant JW Annat, John Oxley Library, State Library of Queensland.

Brisbane General Hospital Casualty Department and Brisbane General Hospital, Graduate Nurses' Association Photographs, John Oxley Library, State Library of Queensland.

Lady Lamington Nurses' Home, The Department of the Environment, Canberra.

Pixie Annat and Bob Hawke, Australian Nursing & Midwifery Federation.

Pixie Annat and Christy Jones, ABC 612, Amanda Dell.

Various family photographs and documents provided by Pixie Annat.

Various St Andrew's War Memorial Hospital photographs provided by St Andrew's War Memorial Hospital.

Centaur recovery, Queensland Department of the Premier and Cabinet, Hugh O'Brien.

Cover image and several photographs of Pixie Annat in 2013–2014, Ray Cash.

Pixie Annat and colleagues at Bancroft Oration, AMA Queensland.

## BIBLIOGRAPHY

Eggleston, Audrey, *My Childhood in Palmwoods: 1930s & 1940s*, Heather Duncan, Queensland, 2005, accessed: Fryer Library, The University of Queensland.

Goodman, Rupert, *Queensland Nurses: Boer War to Vietnam*, Boolarong Publications, Brisbane, 1985.

Gregory, Helen, *A Tradition of Care: A History of Nursing at the Royal Brisbane Hospital*, Boolarong Publications, Brisbane, 1988.

--, *Bearers of Tradition: Nurses of the Royal Brisbane Hospital: 1888–1993,* Boolarong Publications with Royal Brisbane Hospital Graduate Nurses' Association, Brisbane, 1993.

Kerr, Ruth, *A Vision Fulfilled: A History of The Lady Musgrave Trust, 1885–2010,* The Lady Musgrave Trust, Brisbane, 2011.

Krebs, Mollie, *The Palmwoods Story*, Maroochydore, 1972, accessed: Fryer Library, The University of Queensland.

Longhurst, Robert, *Nursing Leadership in Queensland: 50 Years of History (1950–2000),* Directors of Nursing Association Qld Inc, Brisbane, 2000.

Mellick, JSD, *Remembering Them: A History of St Andrew's War Memorial Hospital and its Achievements, 1958–2008,* St Andrew's War Memorial Hospital, Brisbane, 2008.

Palmwoods State Primary School Parents and Citizens Association, *Schooling in Palmwoods: First Hundred Years*, Palmwoods, 1989.

Prior, Deborah, 'Centaur Memorial Fund for Nurses Marks 70', *Australian Nursing Journal*, July 2013, Vol.21(1).

Sommer, Jasmine, *Memoirs of June Nama Sommer 1943–1964: with reference to her work at Nambour Hospital,* Runcorn, 2005, accessed: Fryer Library, The University of Queensland.

Strachan, Glenda, *Labour of Love: The History of the Nurses' Association in Queensland, 1860–1950,* Allen & Unwin, Sydney, 1996.

## ARCHIVES

Unpublished and published documents relating to the history of the Royal Australian Nursing Federation Queensland were accessed using: *Royal Australian Nursing Federation, Queensland Branch Records,* John Oxley Library, State Library of Queensland.

Unpublished and published documents relating to St Andrew's War Memorial Hospital, including copies of *St Andrew's Messenger*, were accessed using: *St Andrew's War Memorial Hospital Records*, UnitingCare Health Archive, Brisbane.

## WEBSITES

Many newspaper and magazine articles were accessed via the National Library of Australia Trove portal, http://trove.nla.gov.au

**Other websites accessed included:**

AHS Centaur Association, www.centaur.org.au

AIF Project, www.aif.adfa.edu.au

ANZAC Day, www.anzacday.org.au

Australian Dictionary of Biography, adb.anu.edu.au

Australian Nursing & Midwifery Federation, www.anmf.org.au

Australian War Memorial, www.awm.gov.au

Digger History, www.diggerhistory.info

Internet Archive Digital Library, www.archive.org

Queensland Nurses' Union, www.qnu.org.au

Queensland Places, www.queenslandplaces.com.au/palmwoods

Queensland War Memorial Register, www.qldwarmemorials.com.au

# Index

**COLLEEN RYAN CLUR** has worked as a journalist and editor in South Africa and as a senior communications practitioner in Australia. She has also worked in executive communication and marketing roles for The University of Queensland and Queensland University of Technology. Her passions are writing and history.

Colleen is the author of the biography *Beyers Naude: Pilgrimage of Faith*, about the life of an acclaimed anti-apartheid leader in South Africa. She has a Master of Arts (History) and a Graduate Diploma in Business Administration, and is managing director of Compass Communications Group.